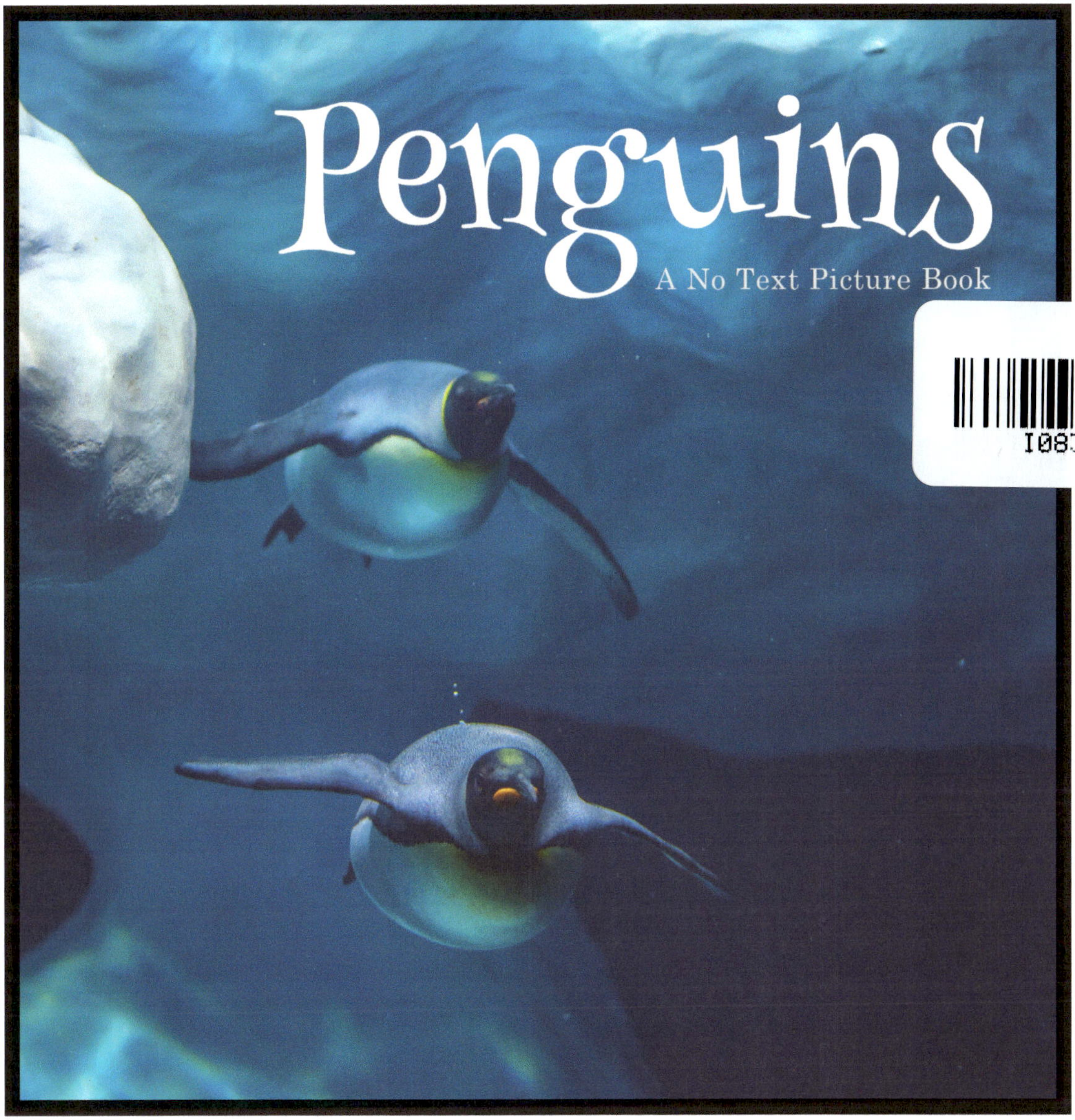

Penguins

A No Text Picture Book

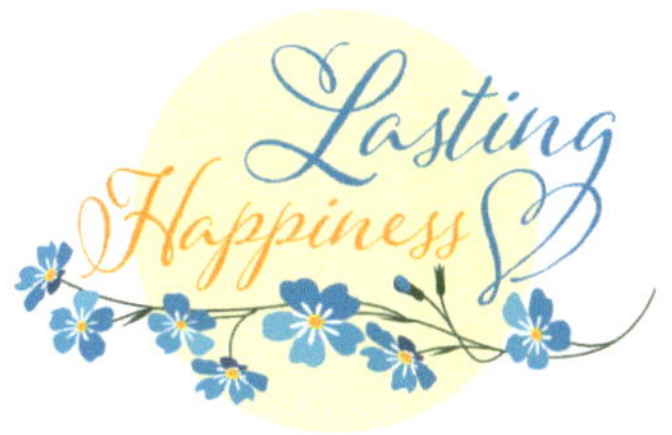

ISBN: 9798421480198

To:

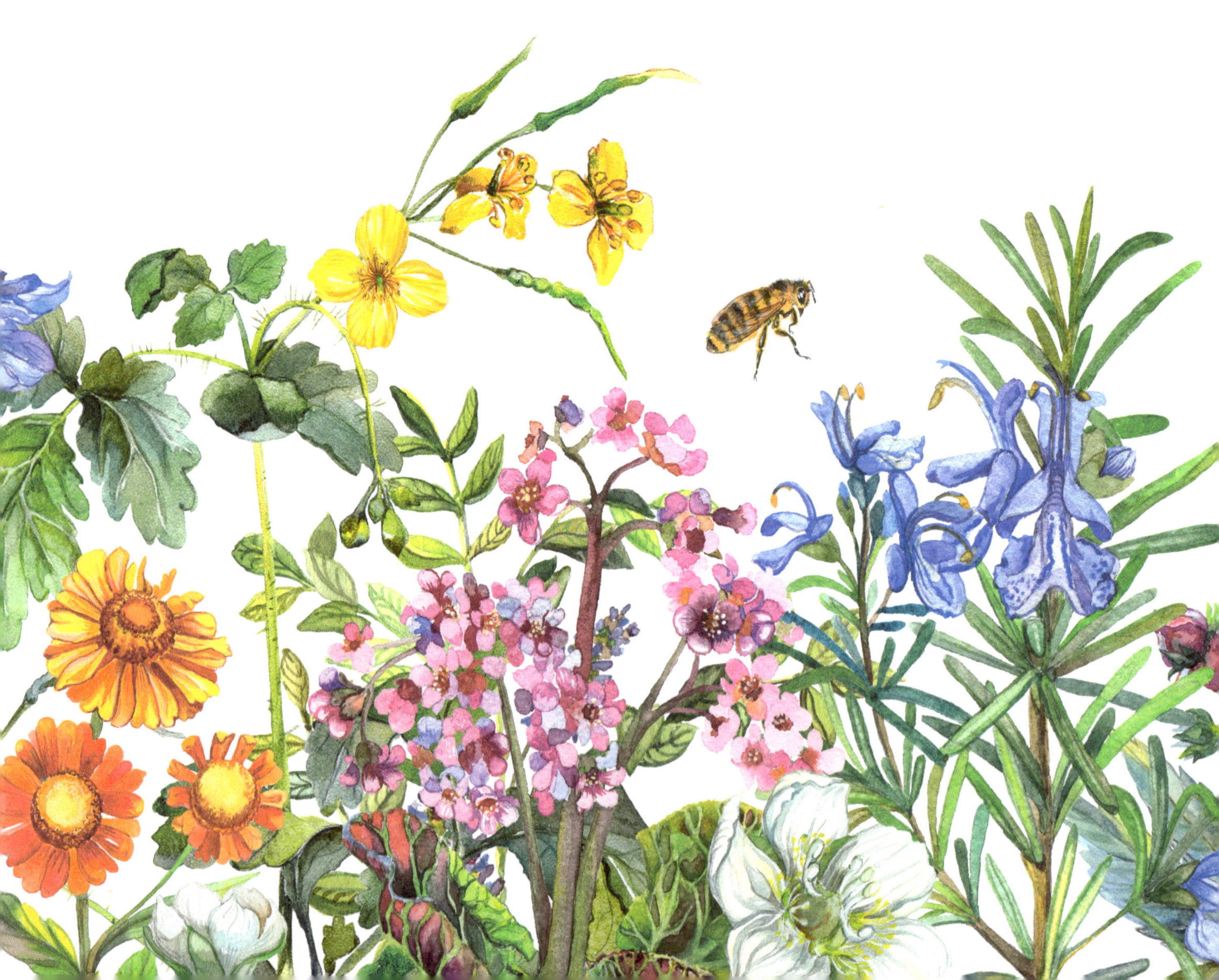

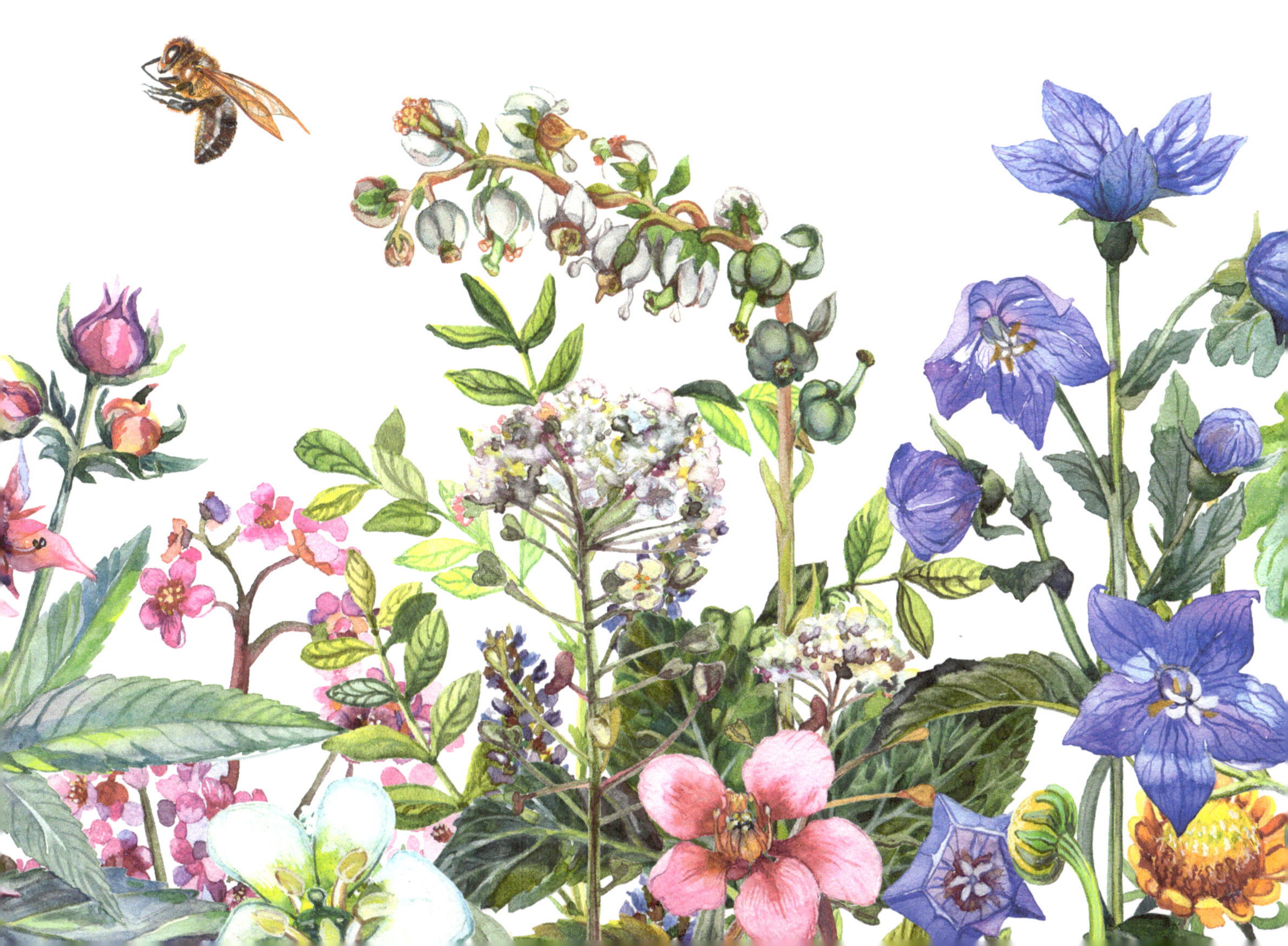

FROM:

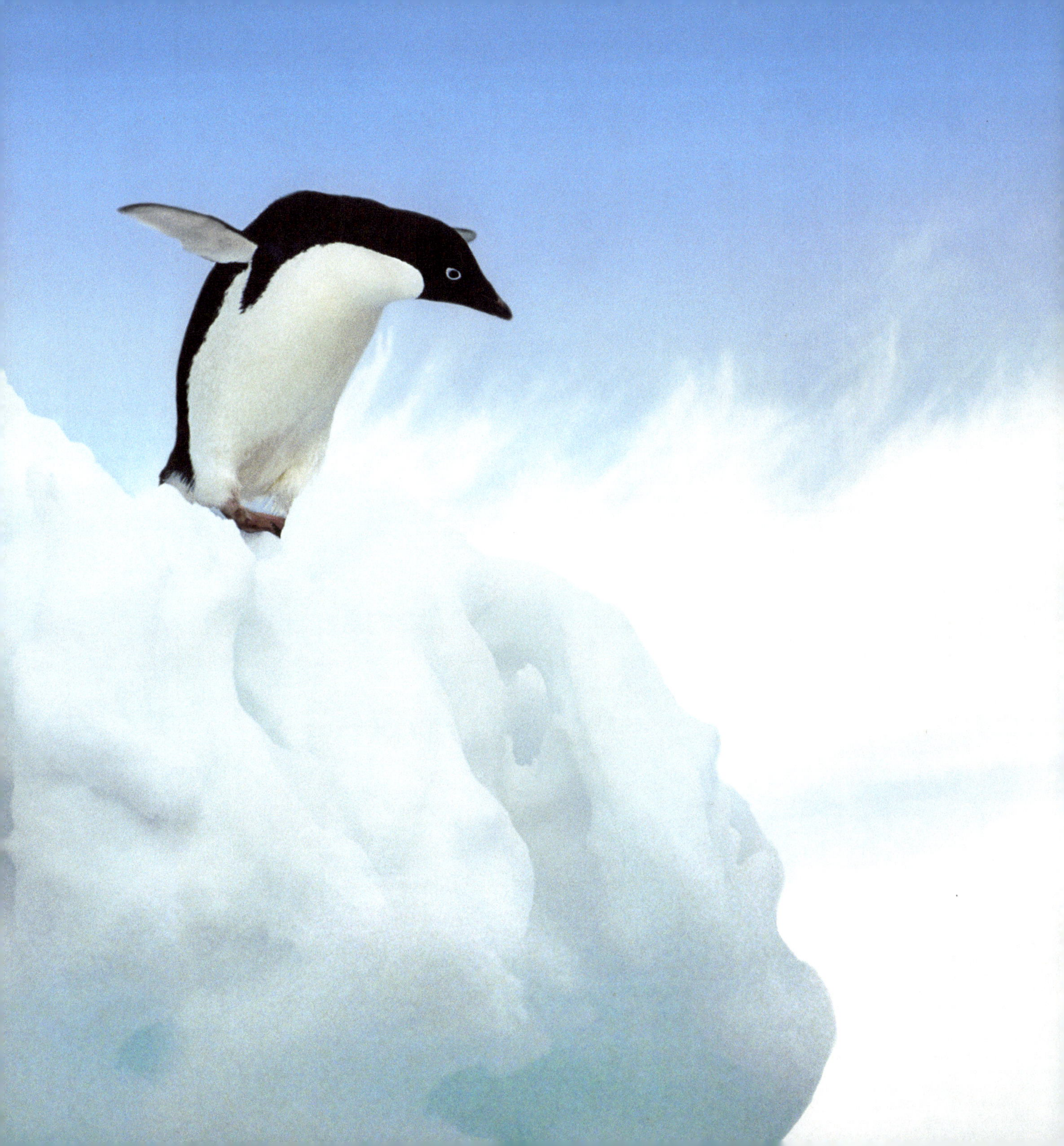

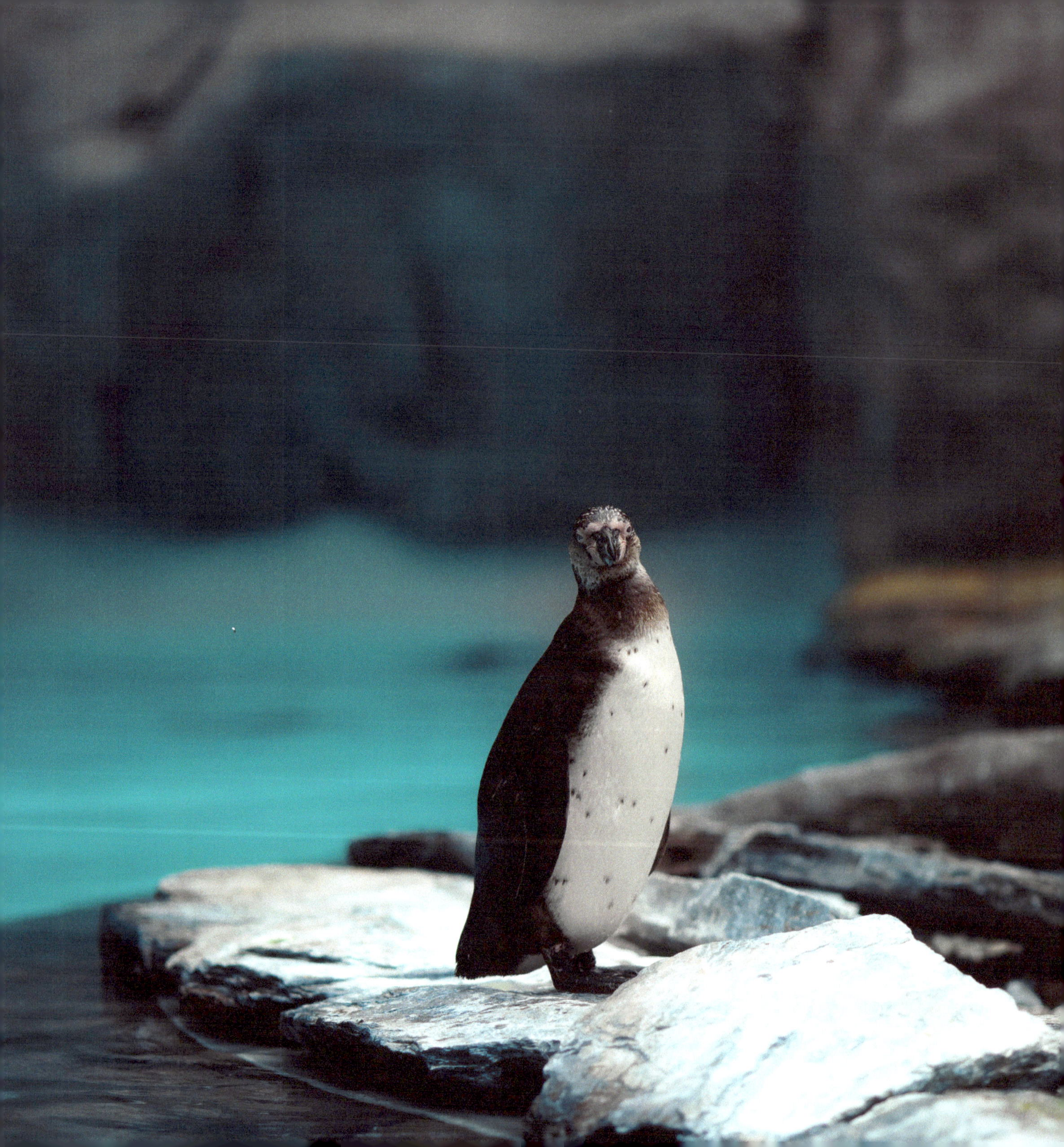

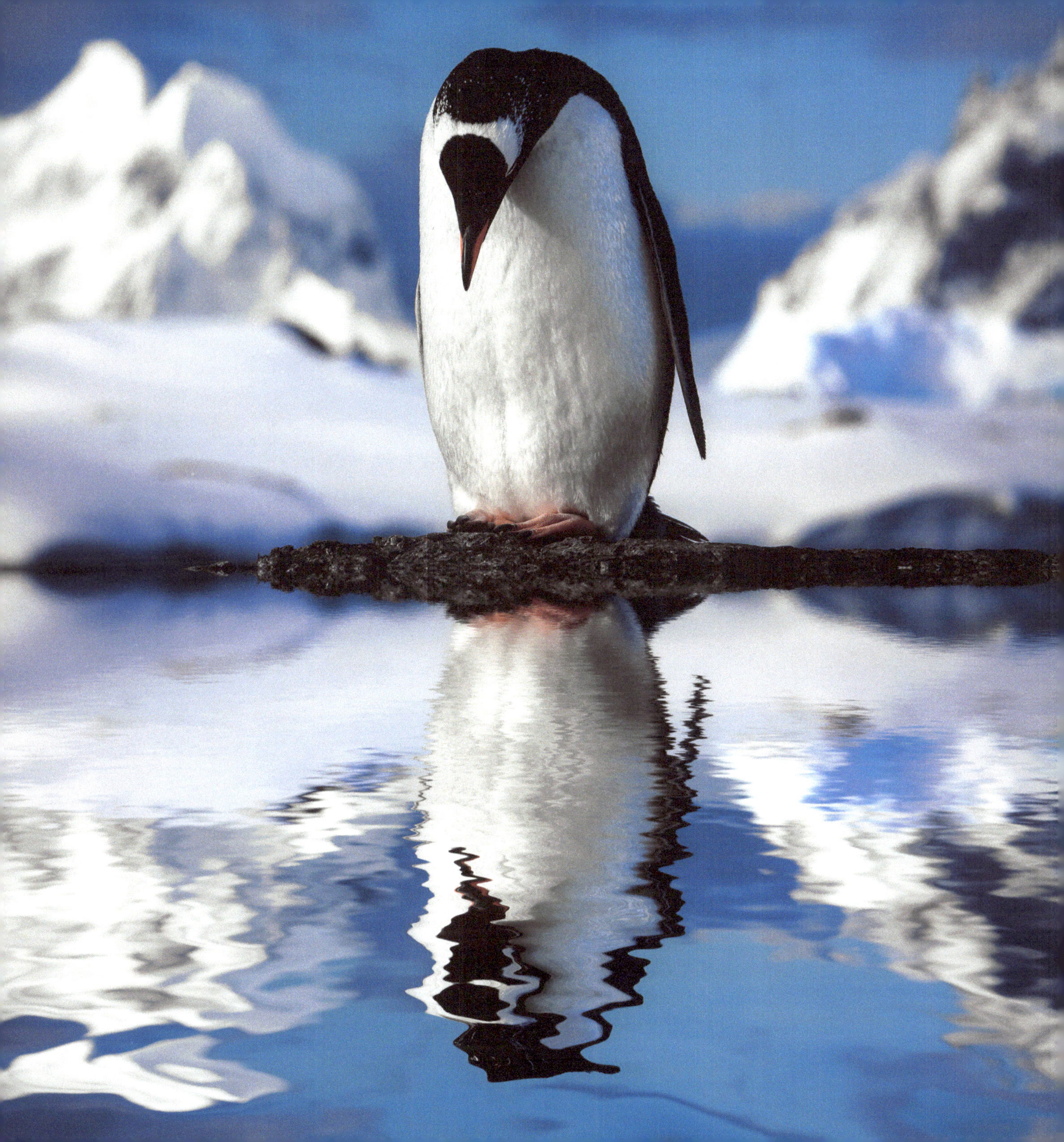

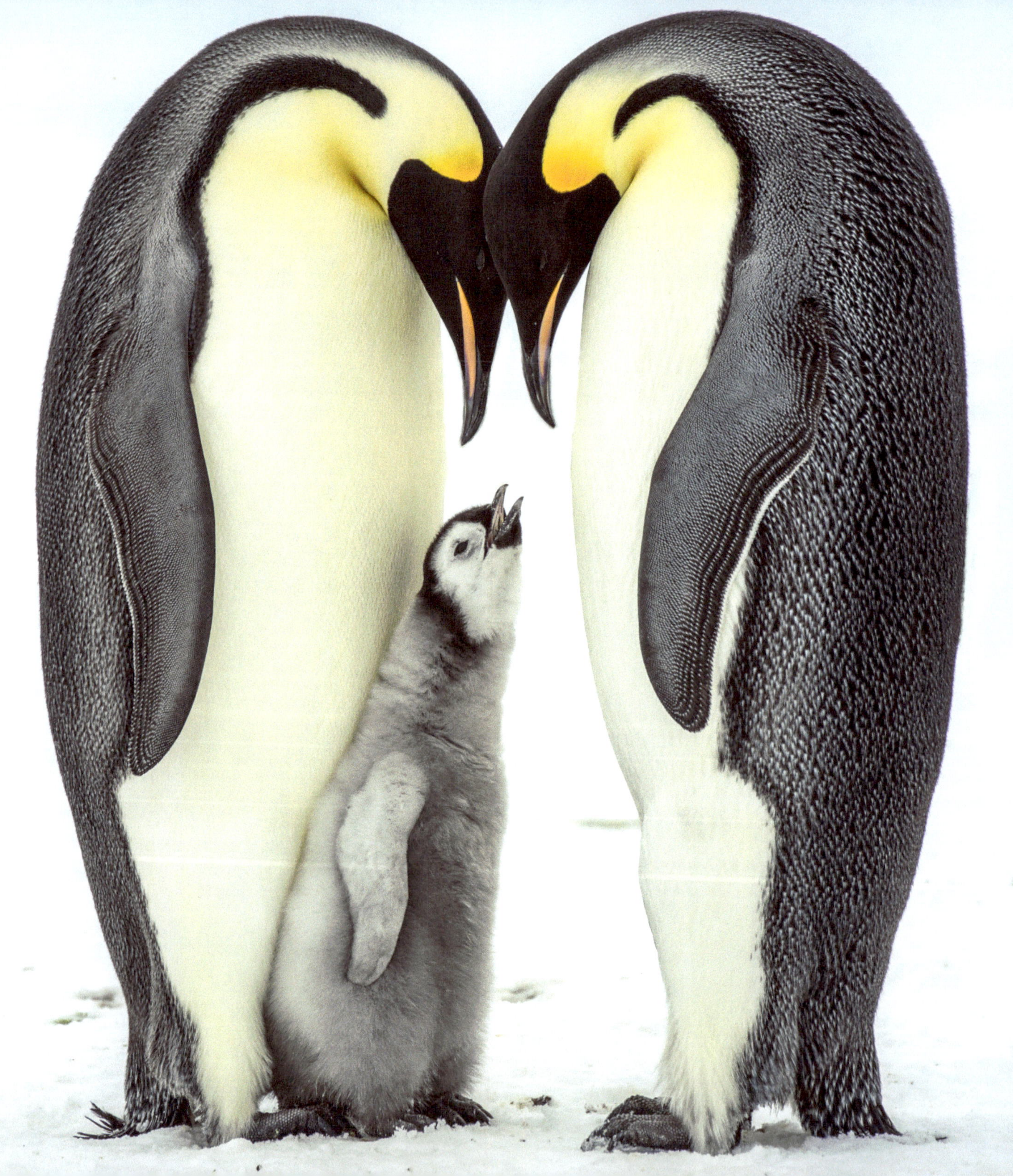

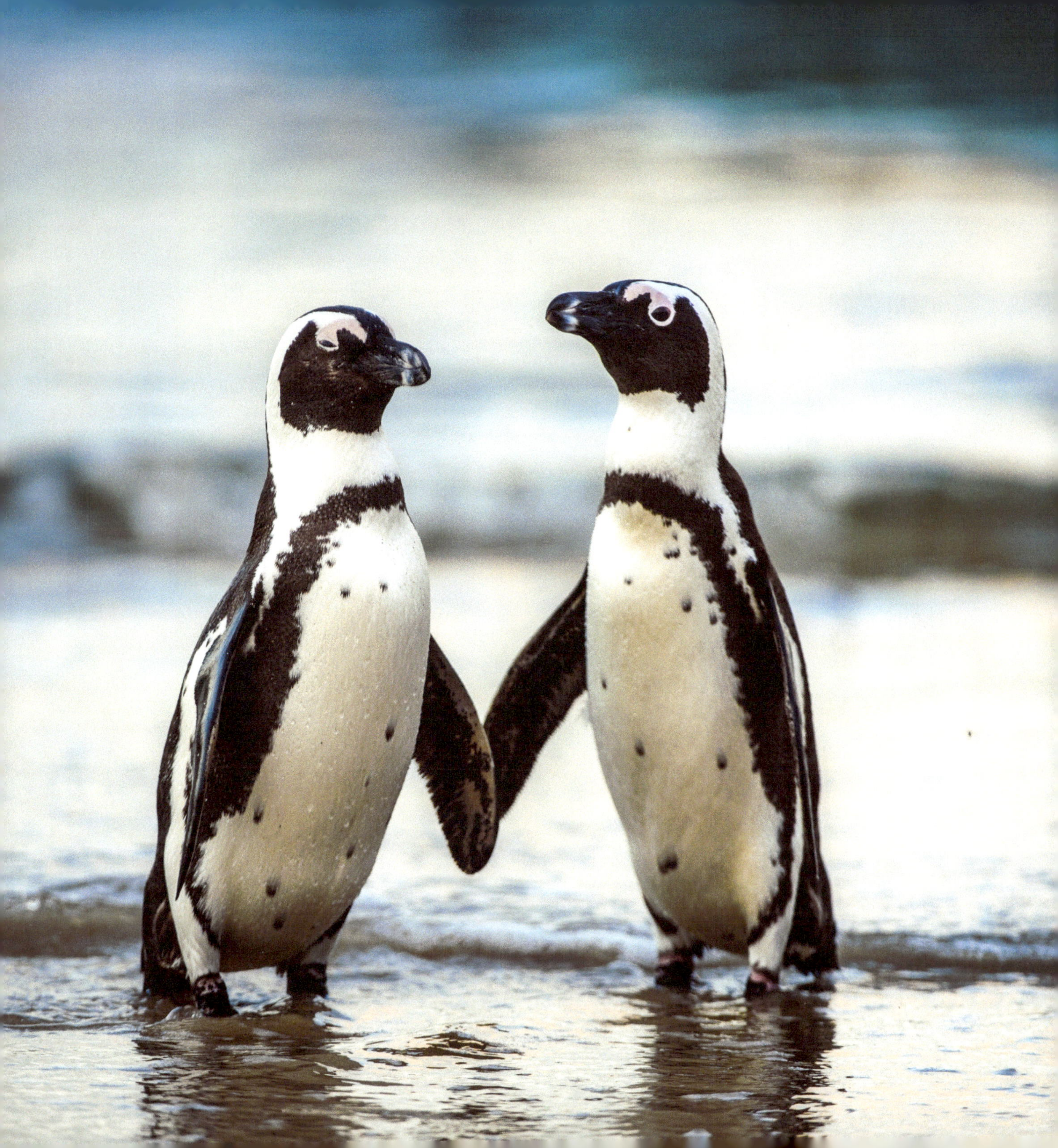

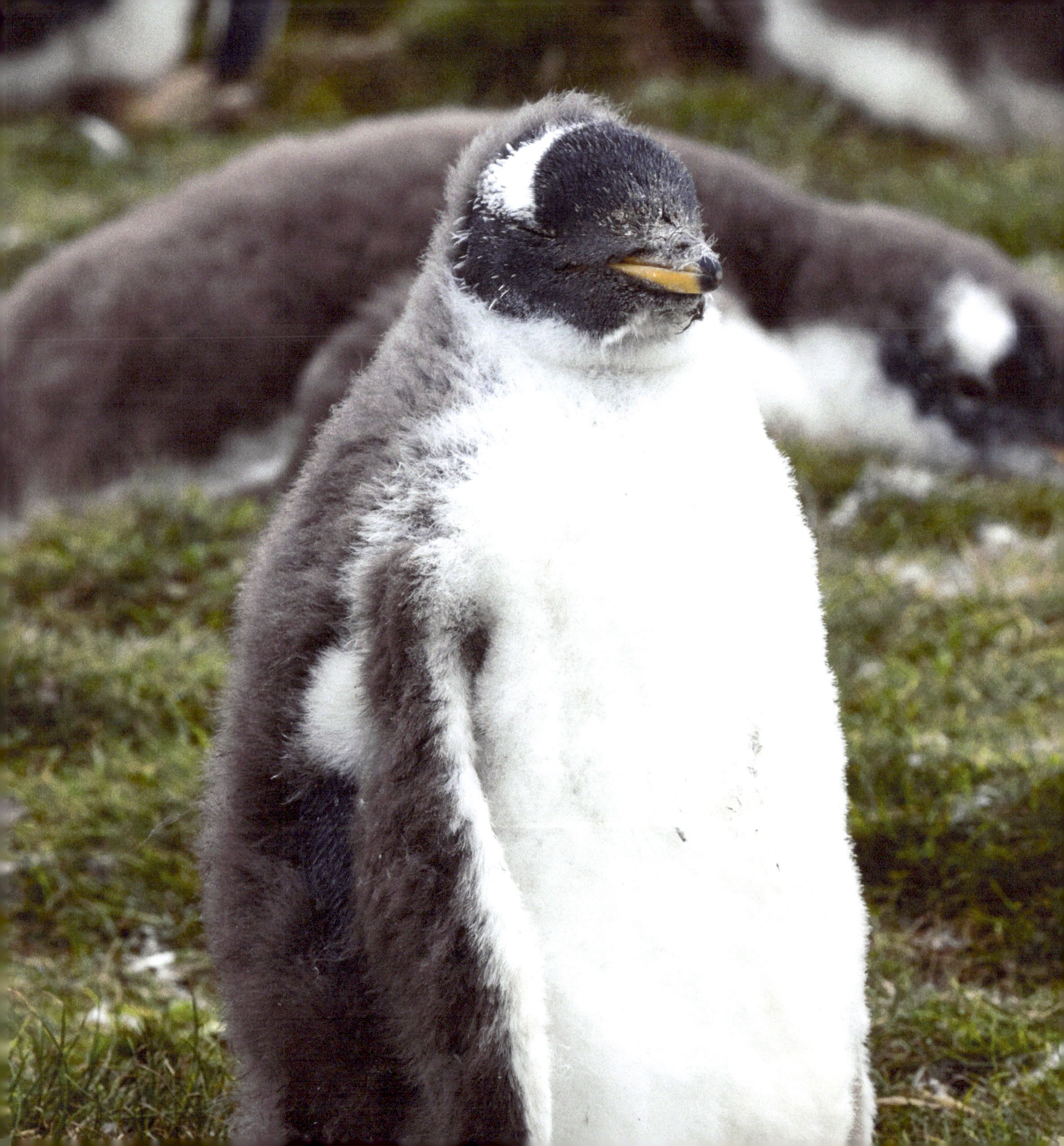

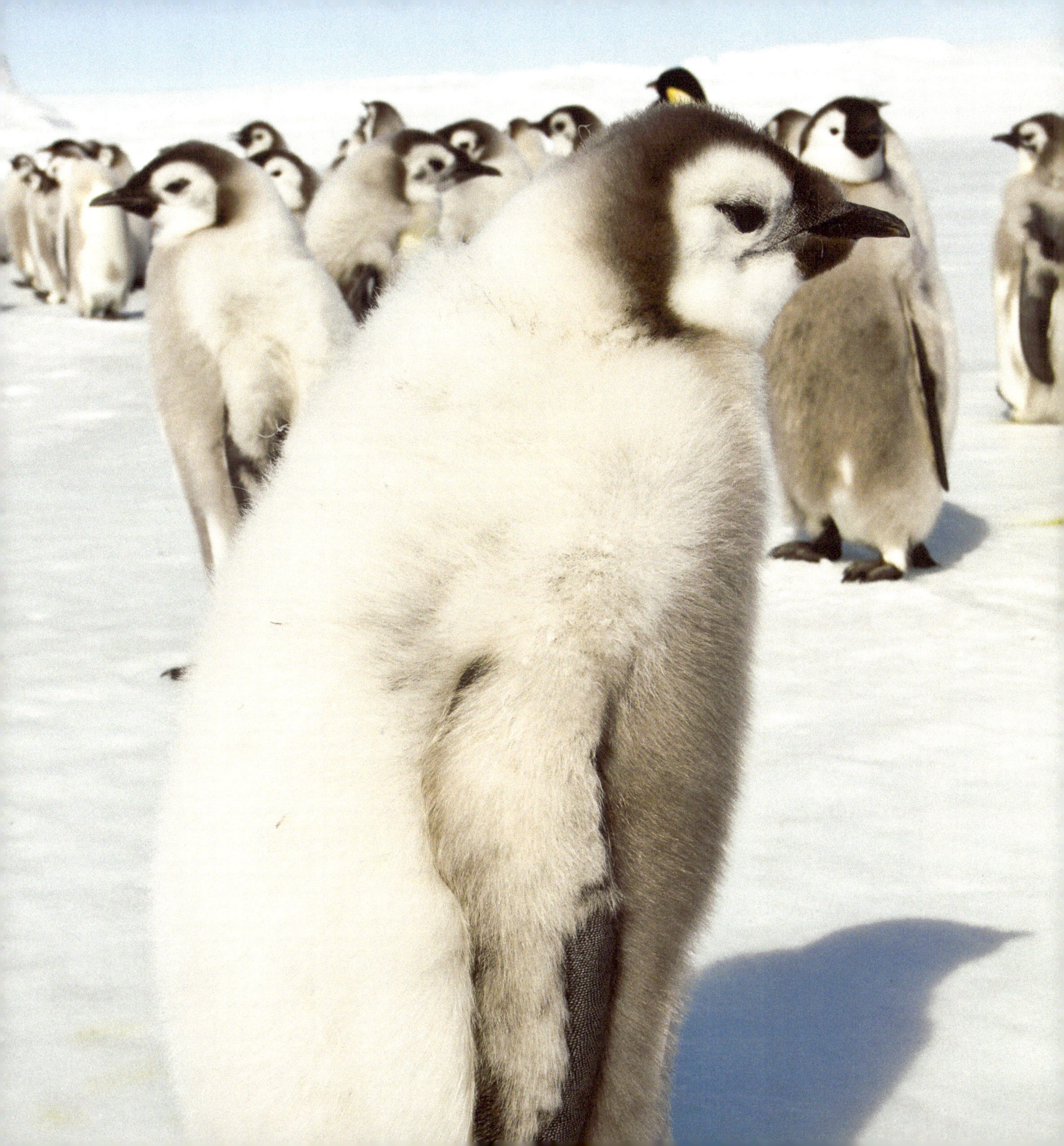

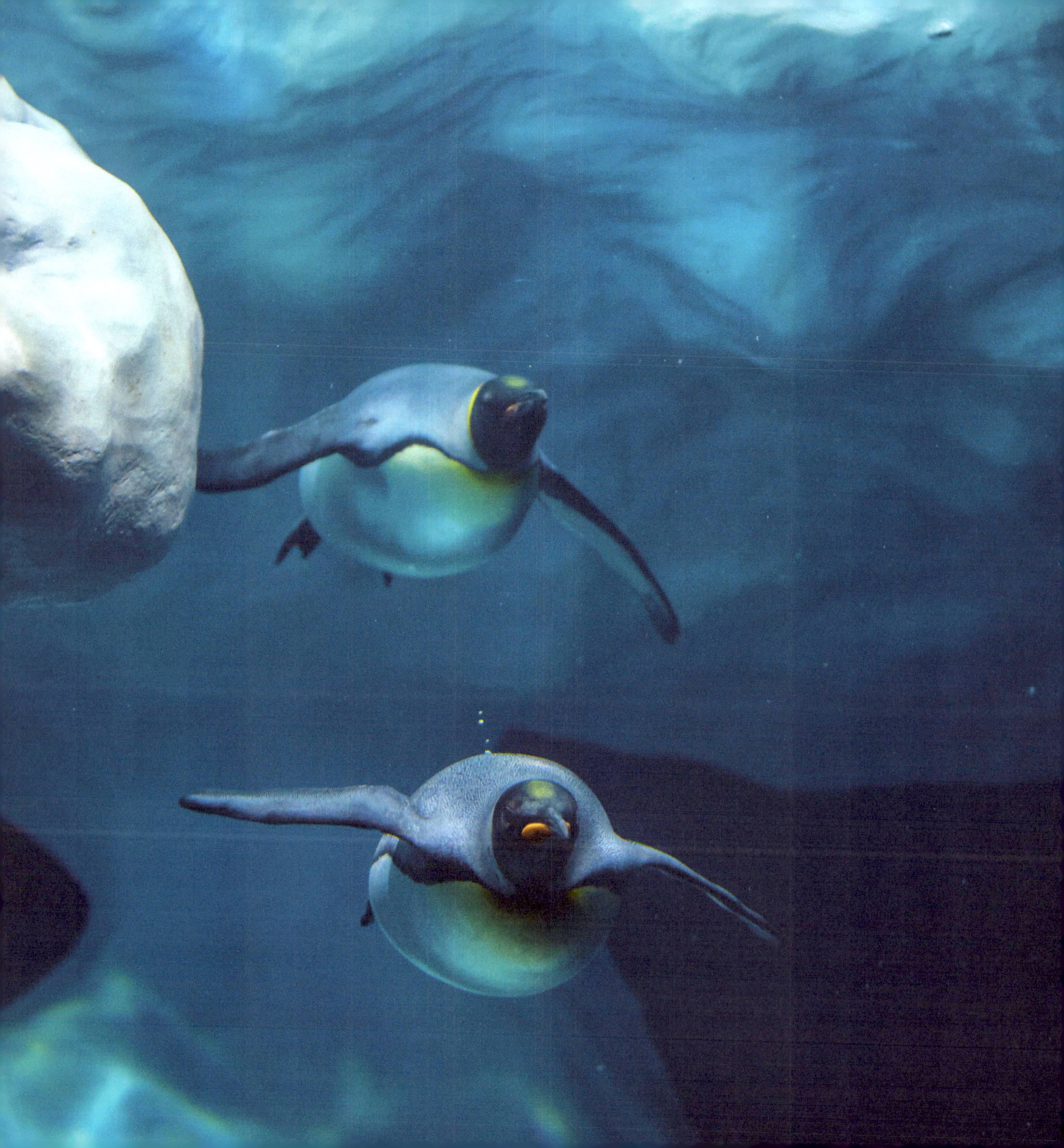

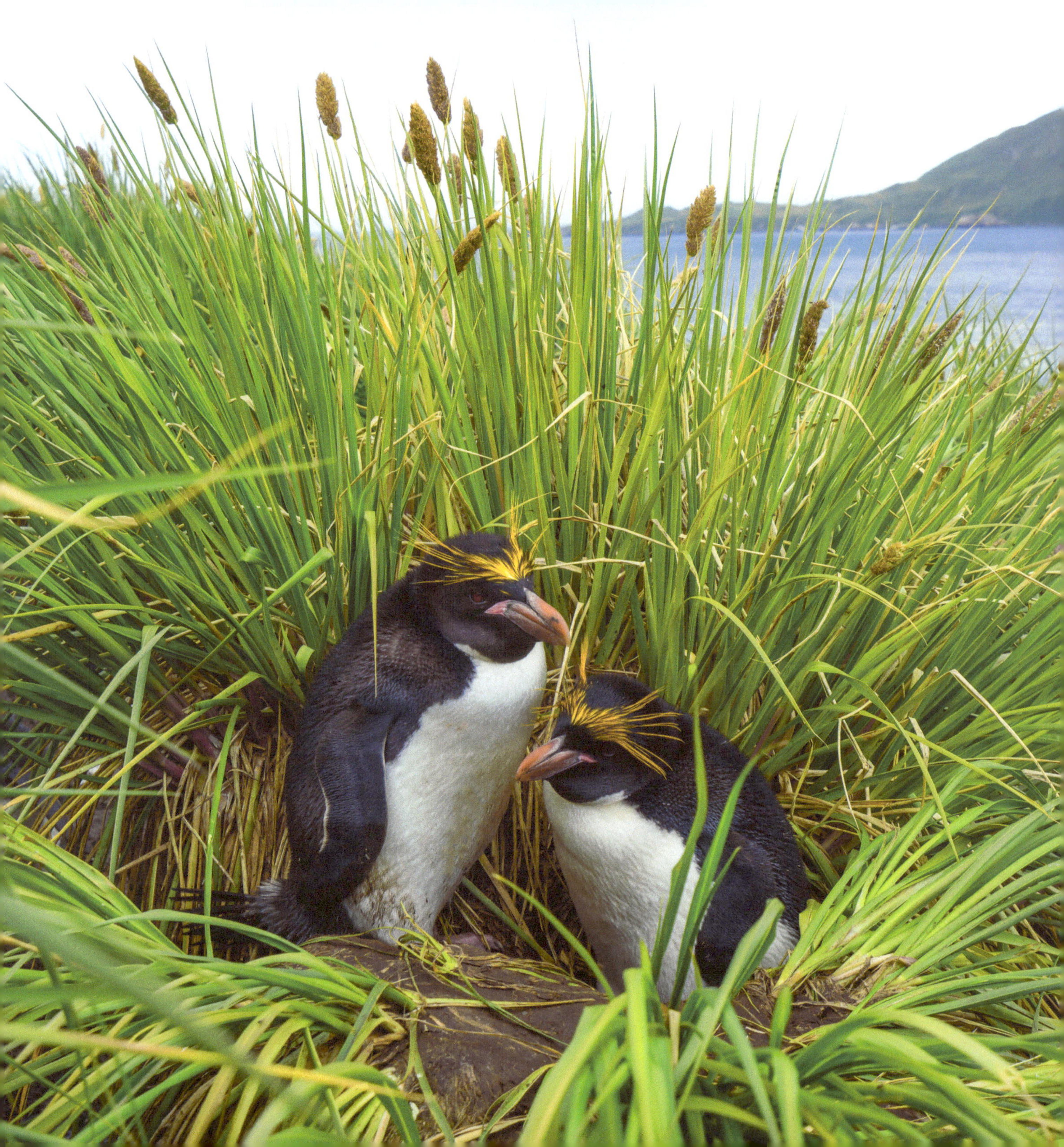

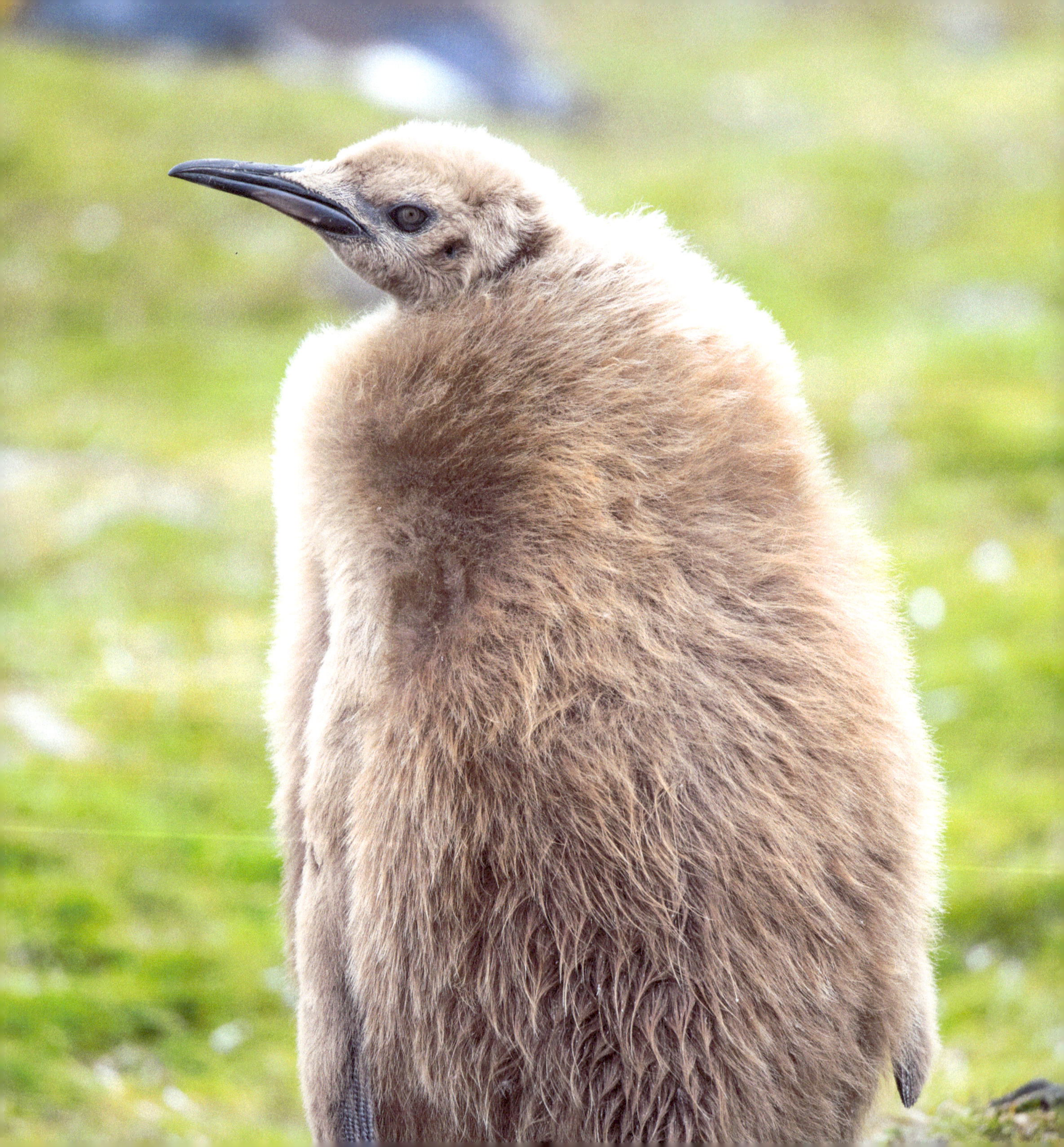

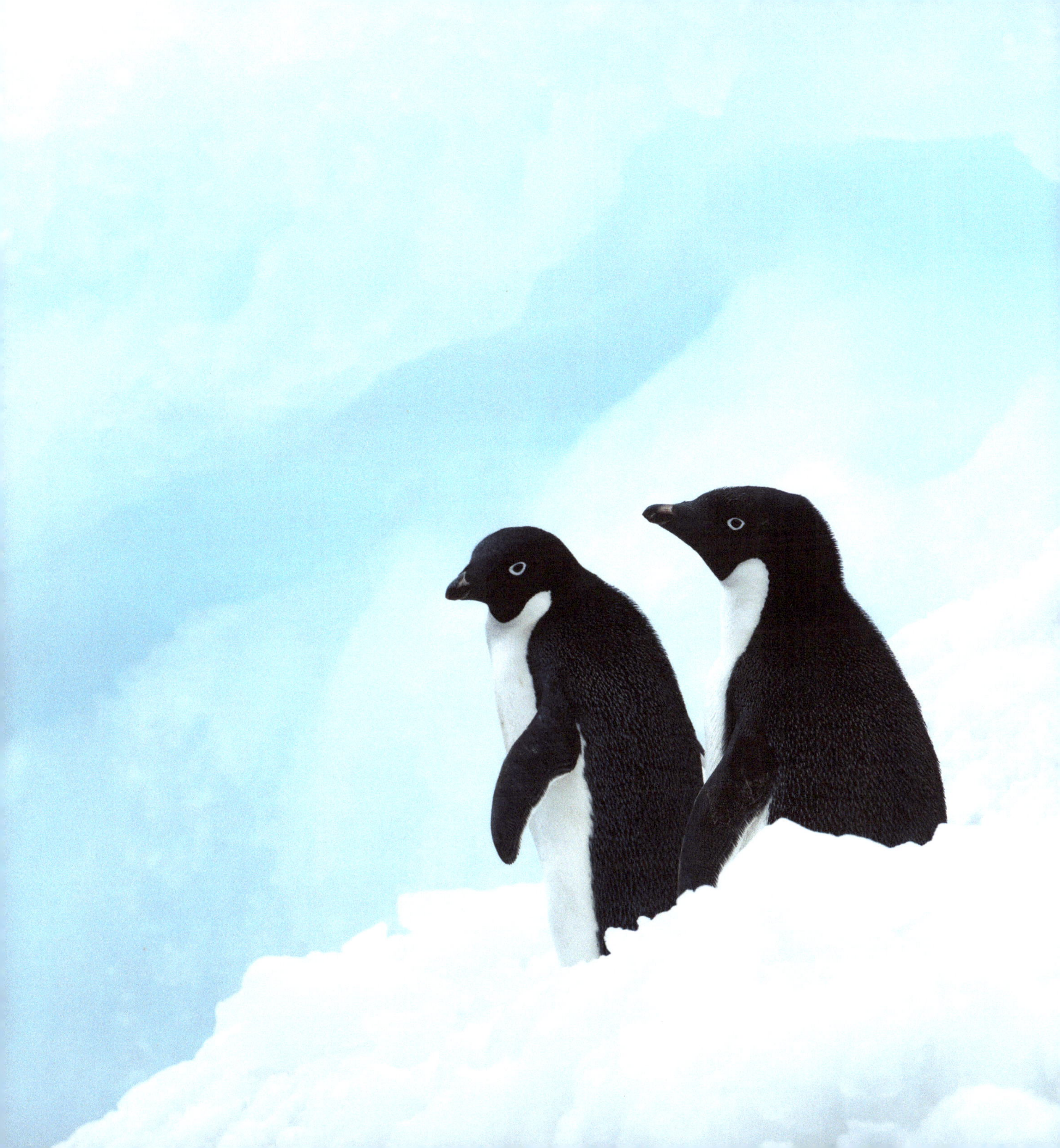

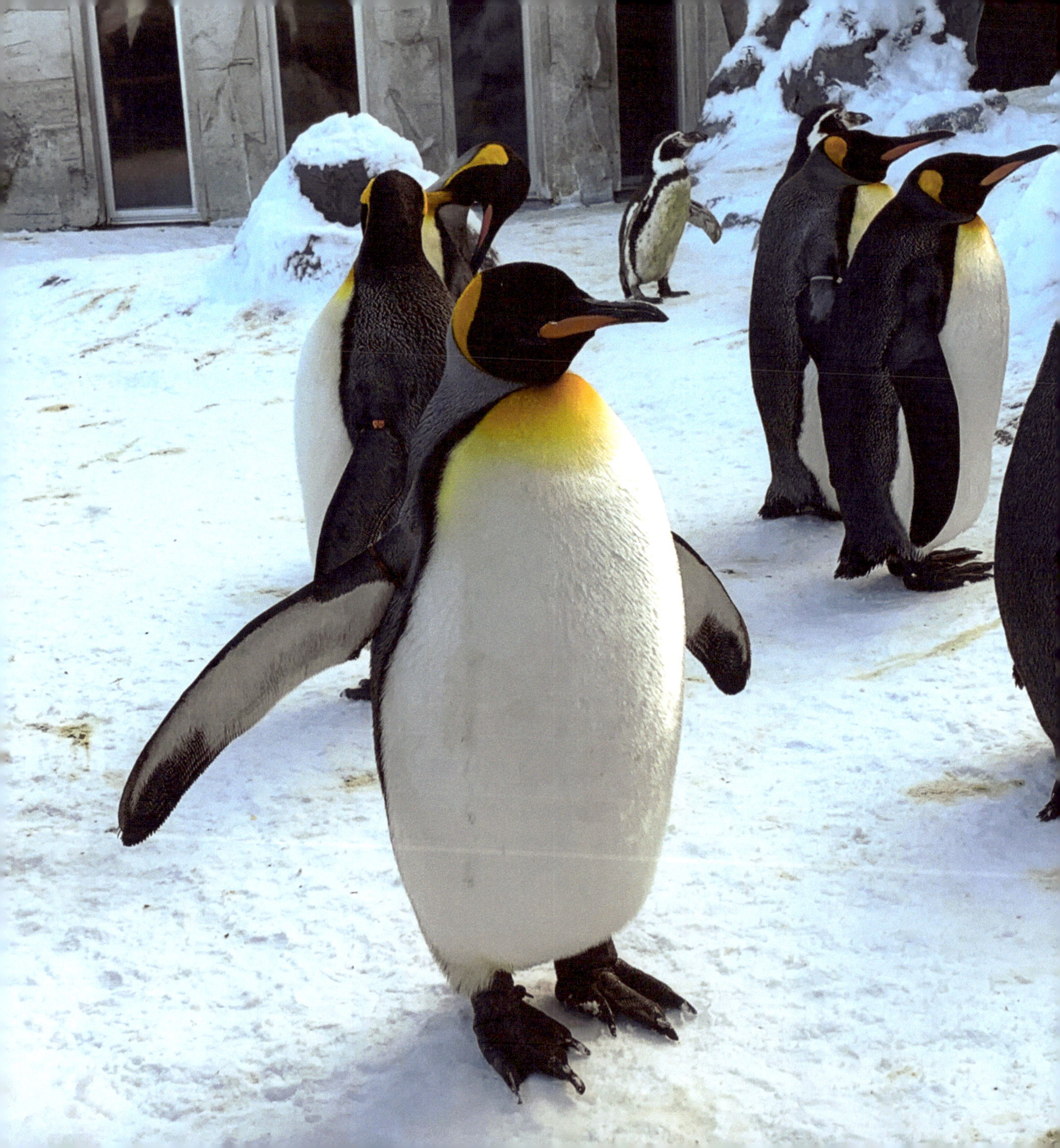

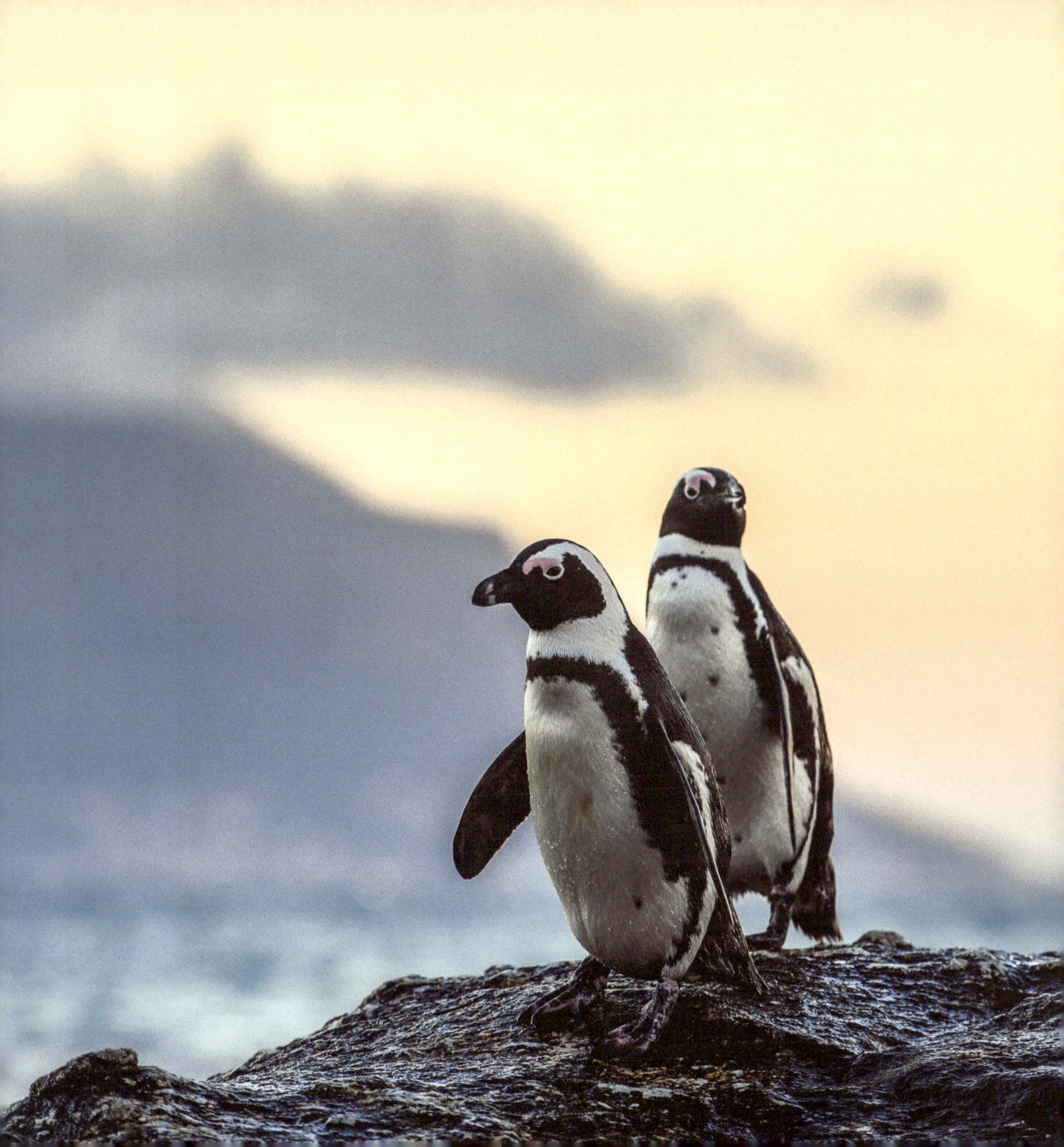

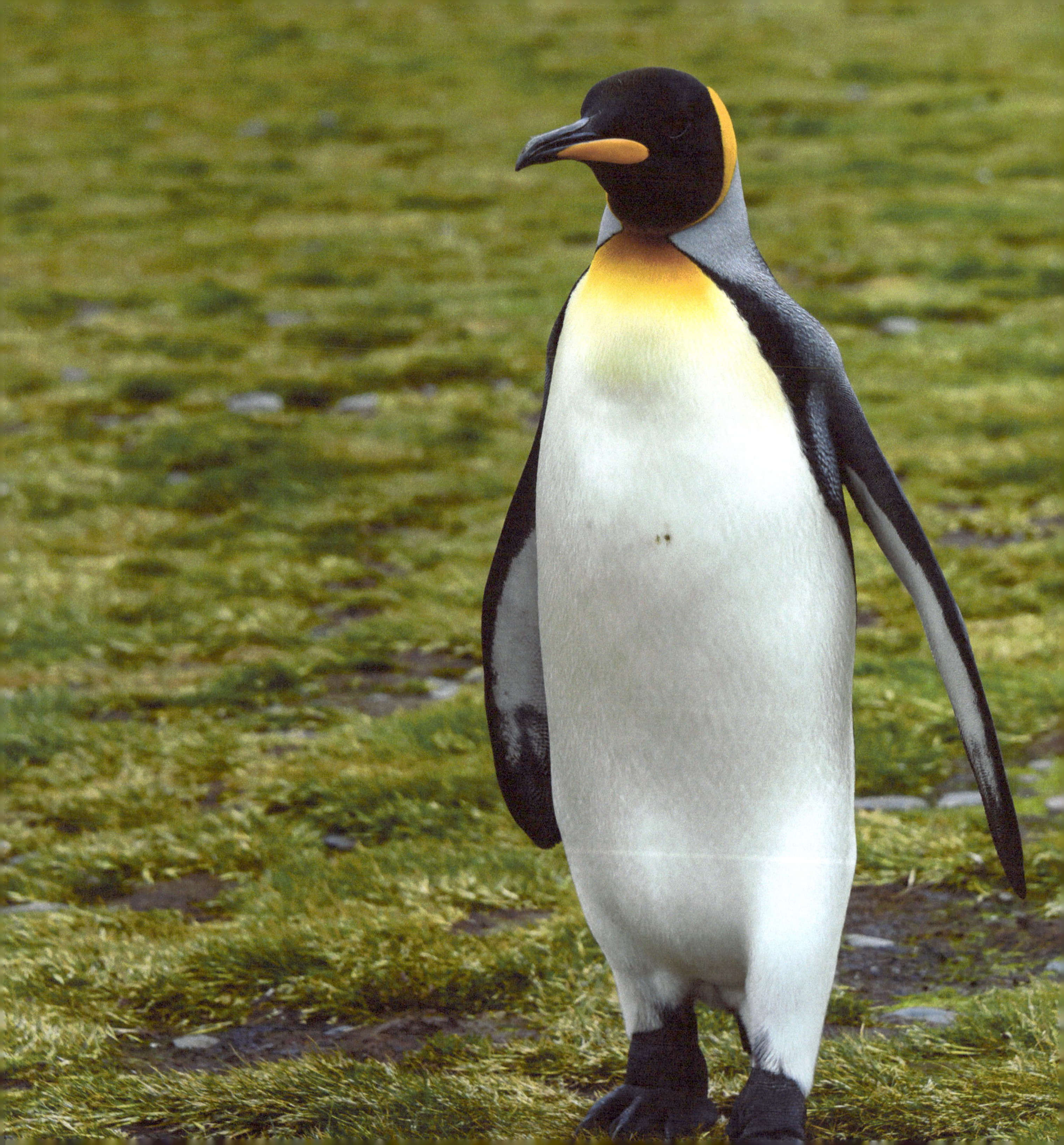

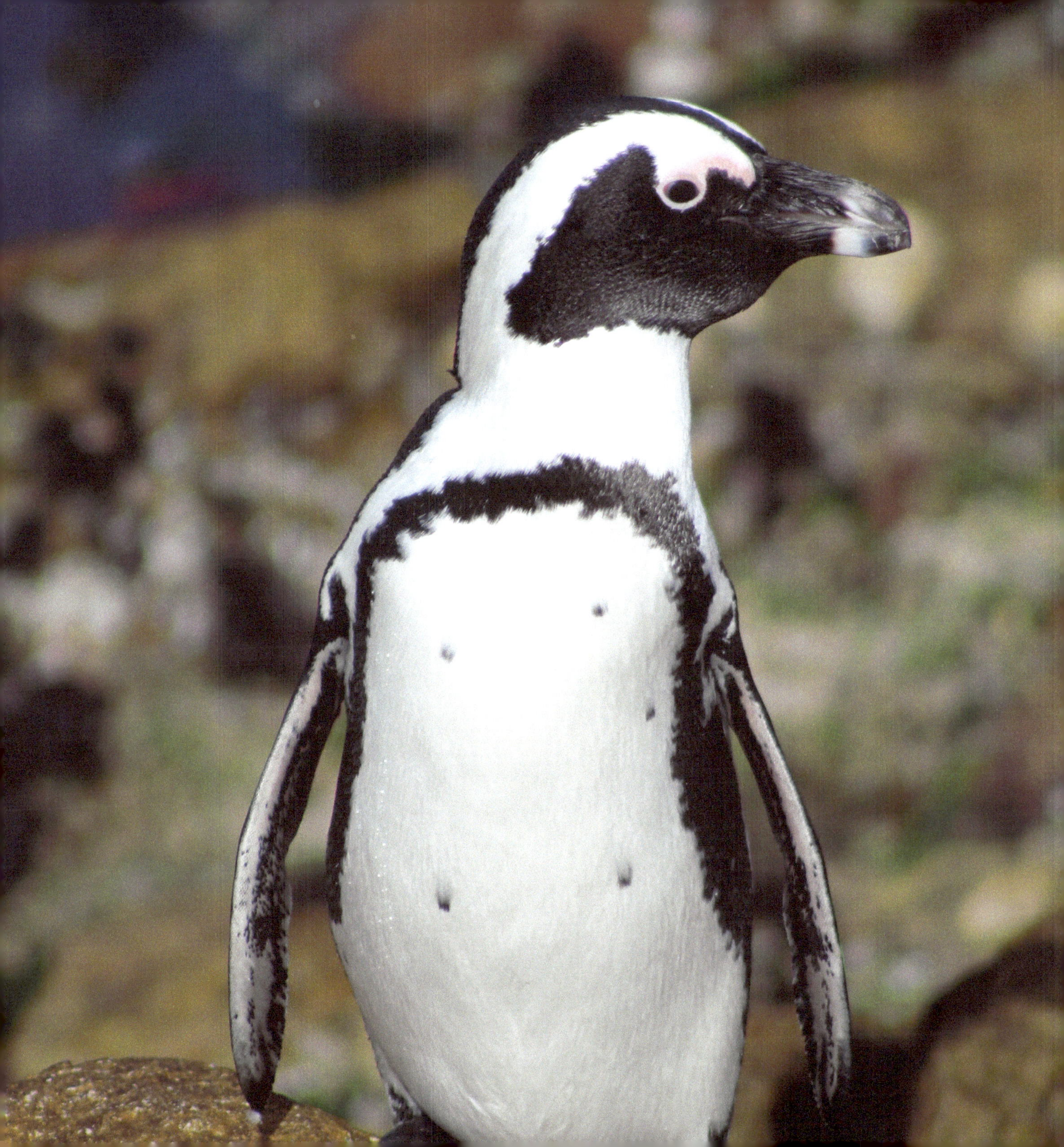

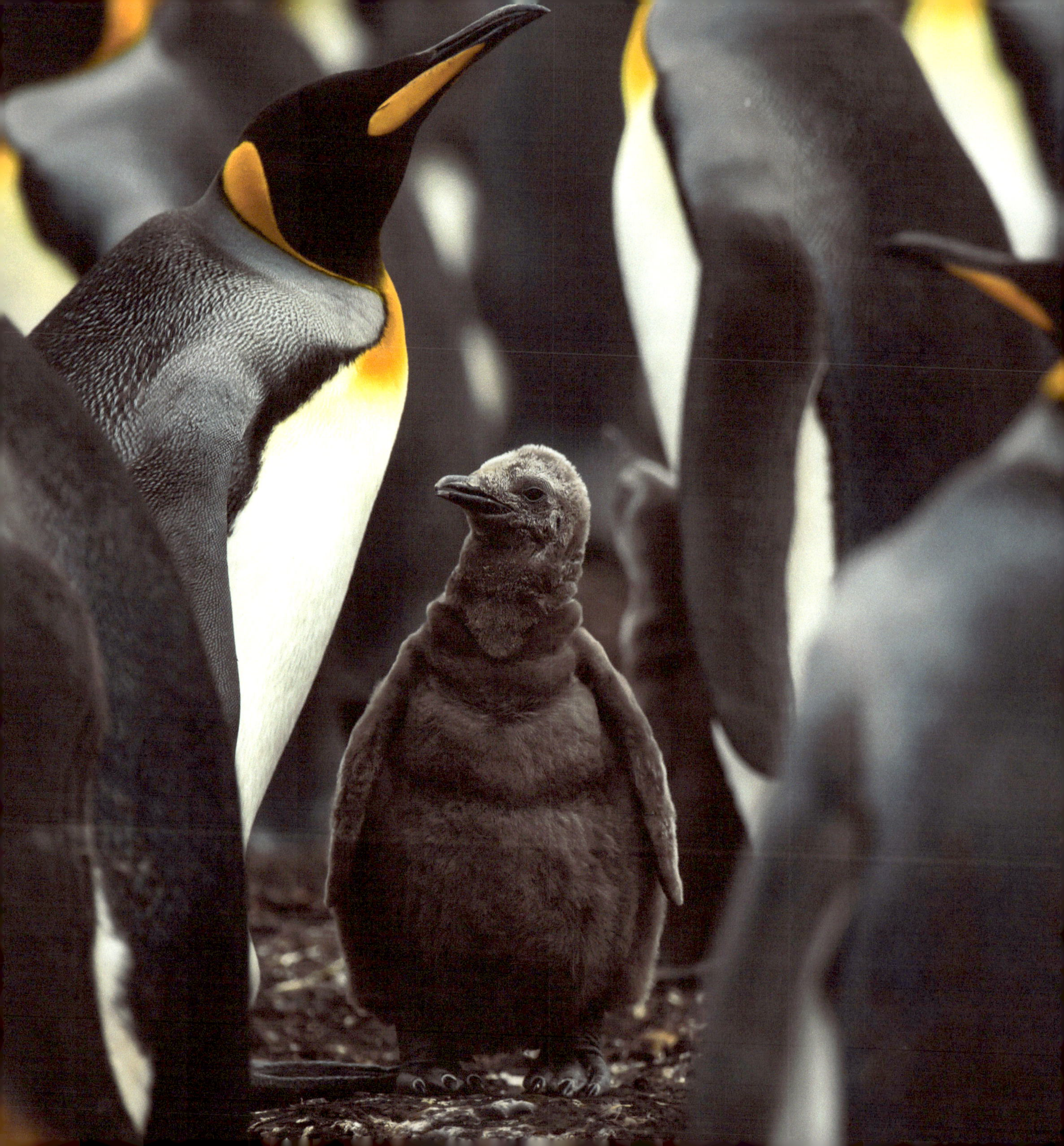

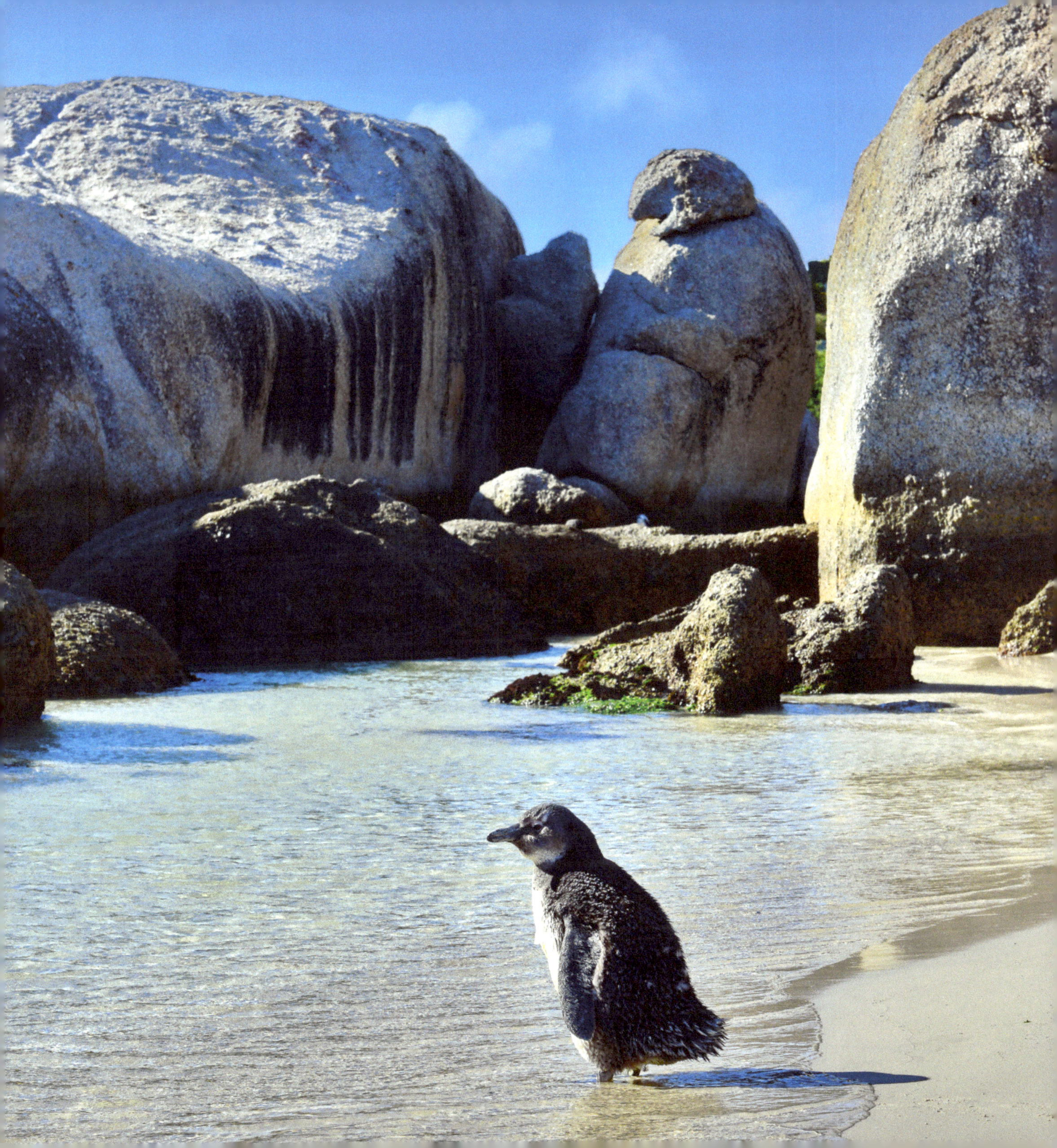

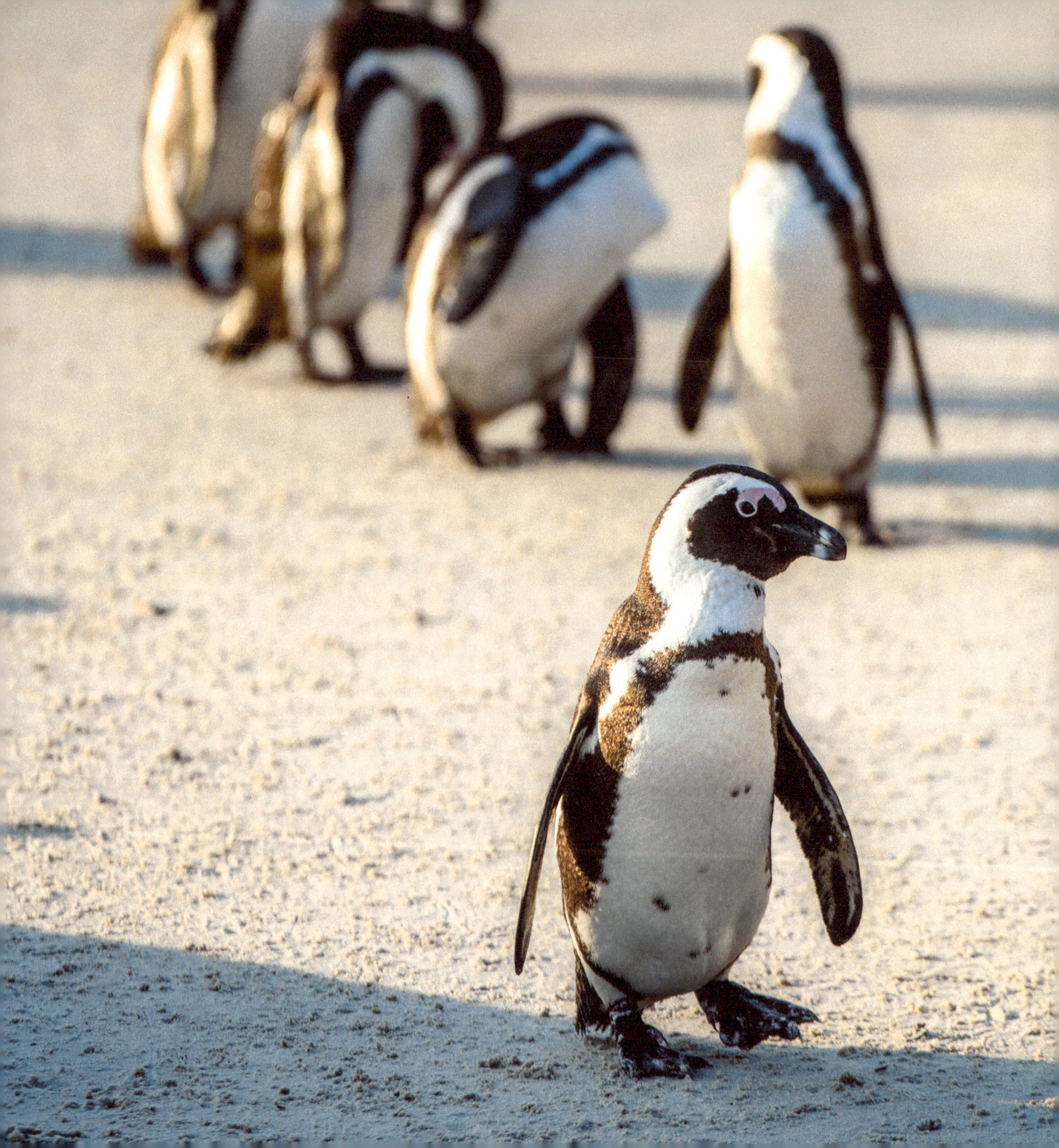

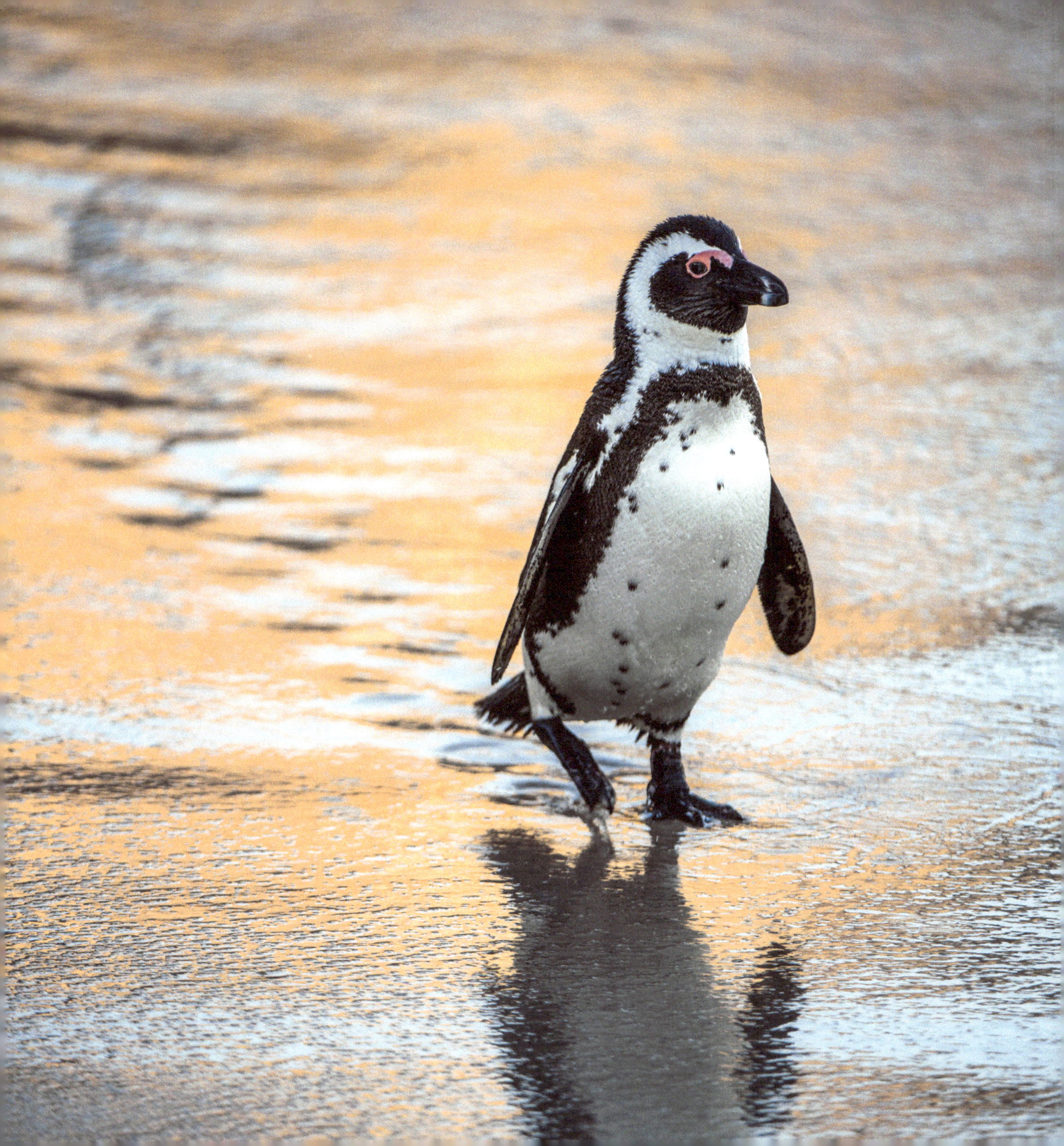

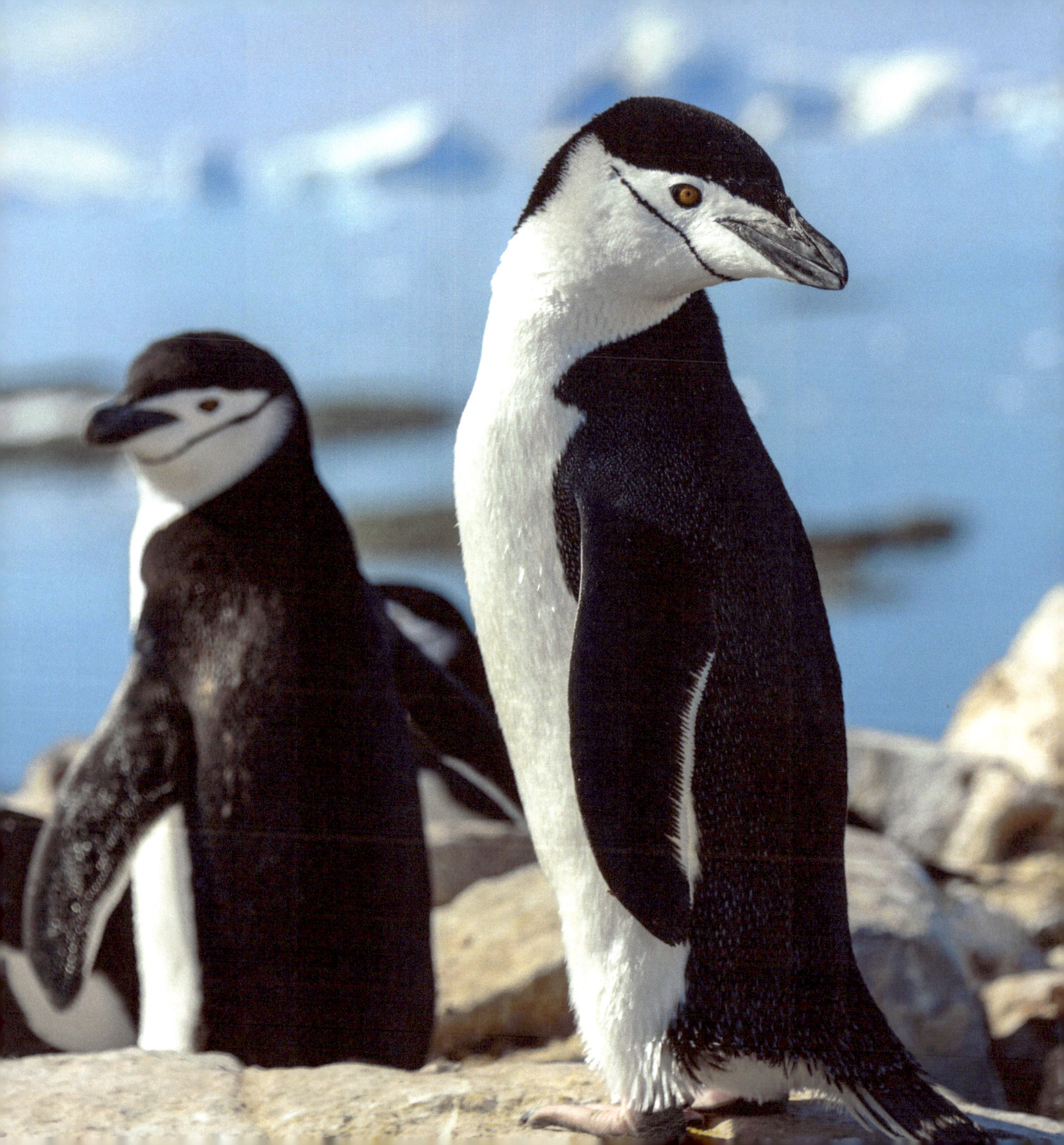

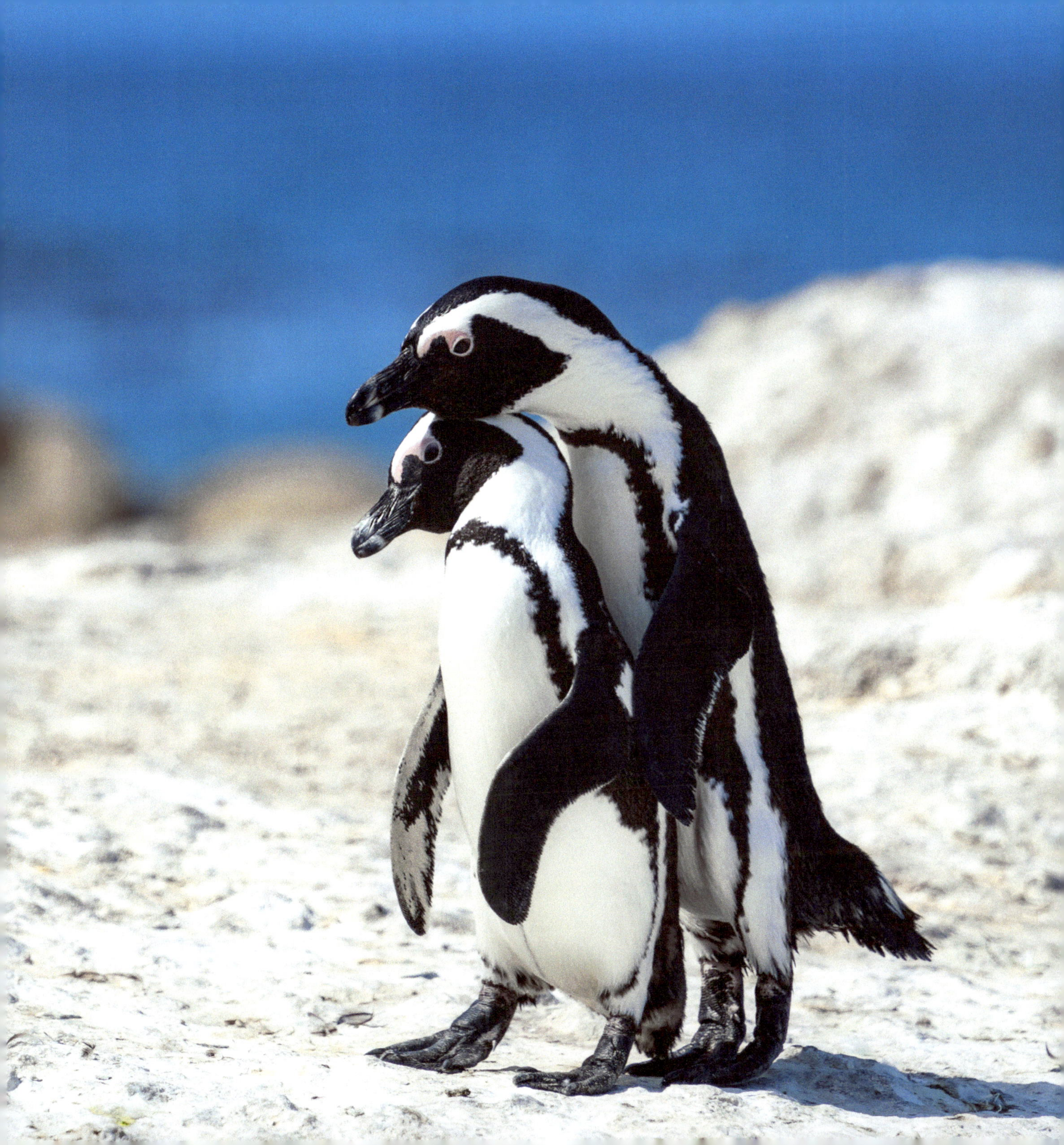

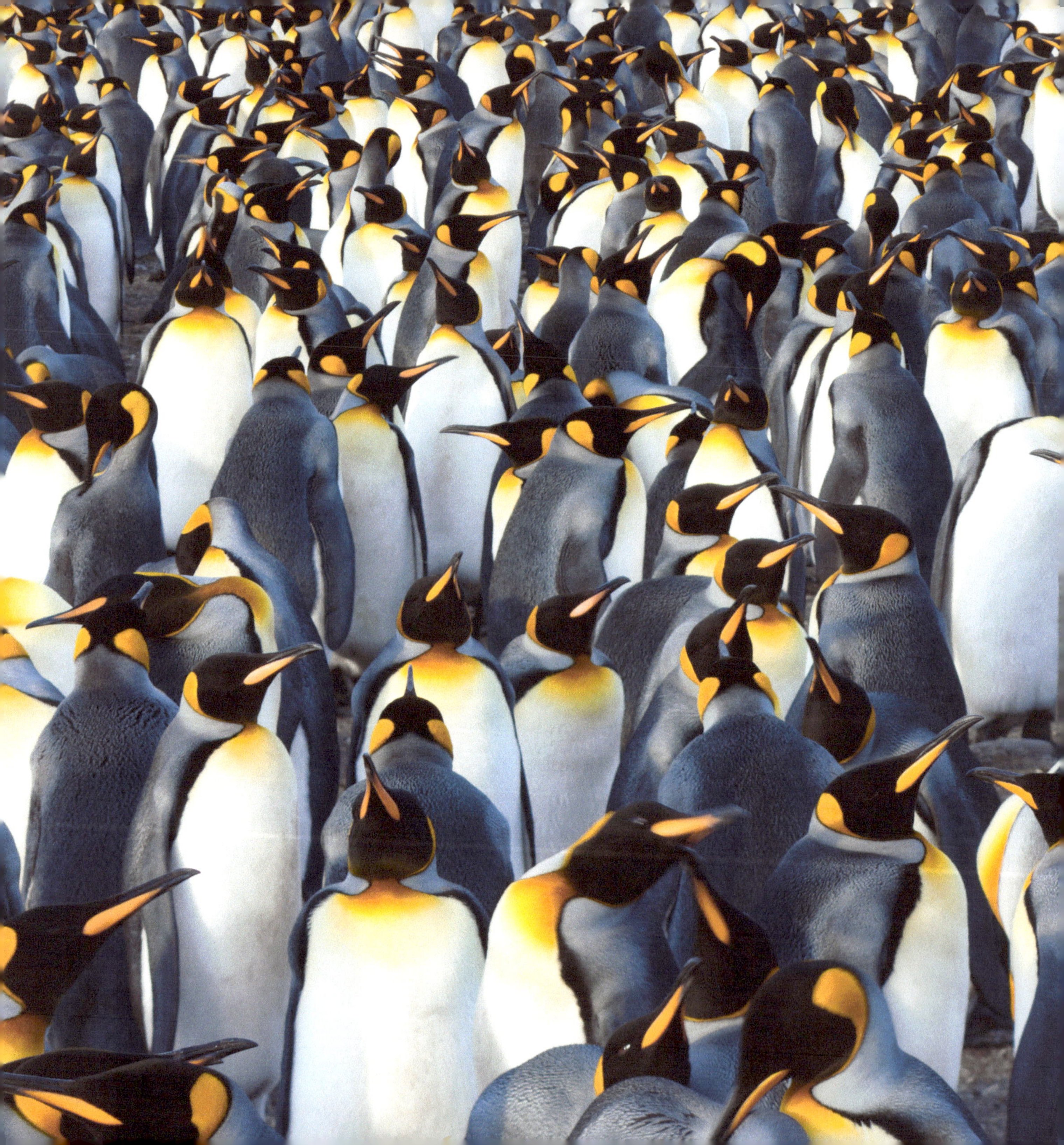

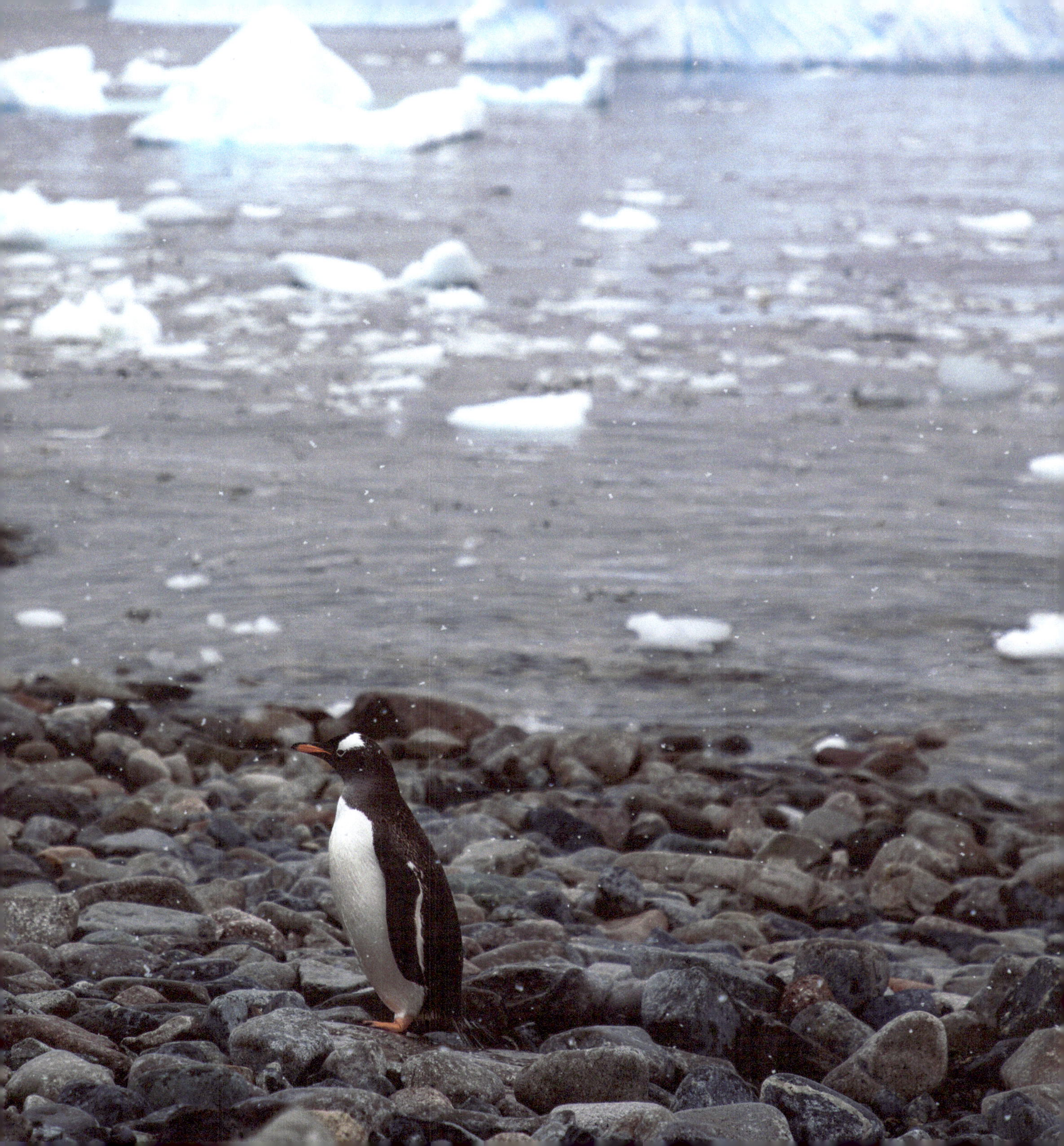

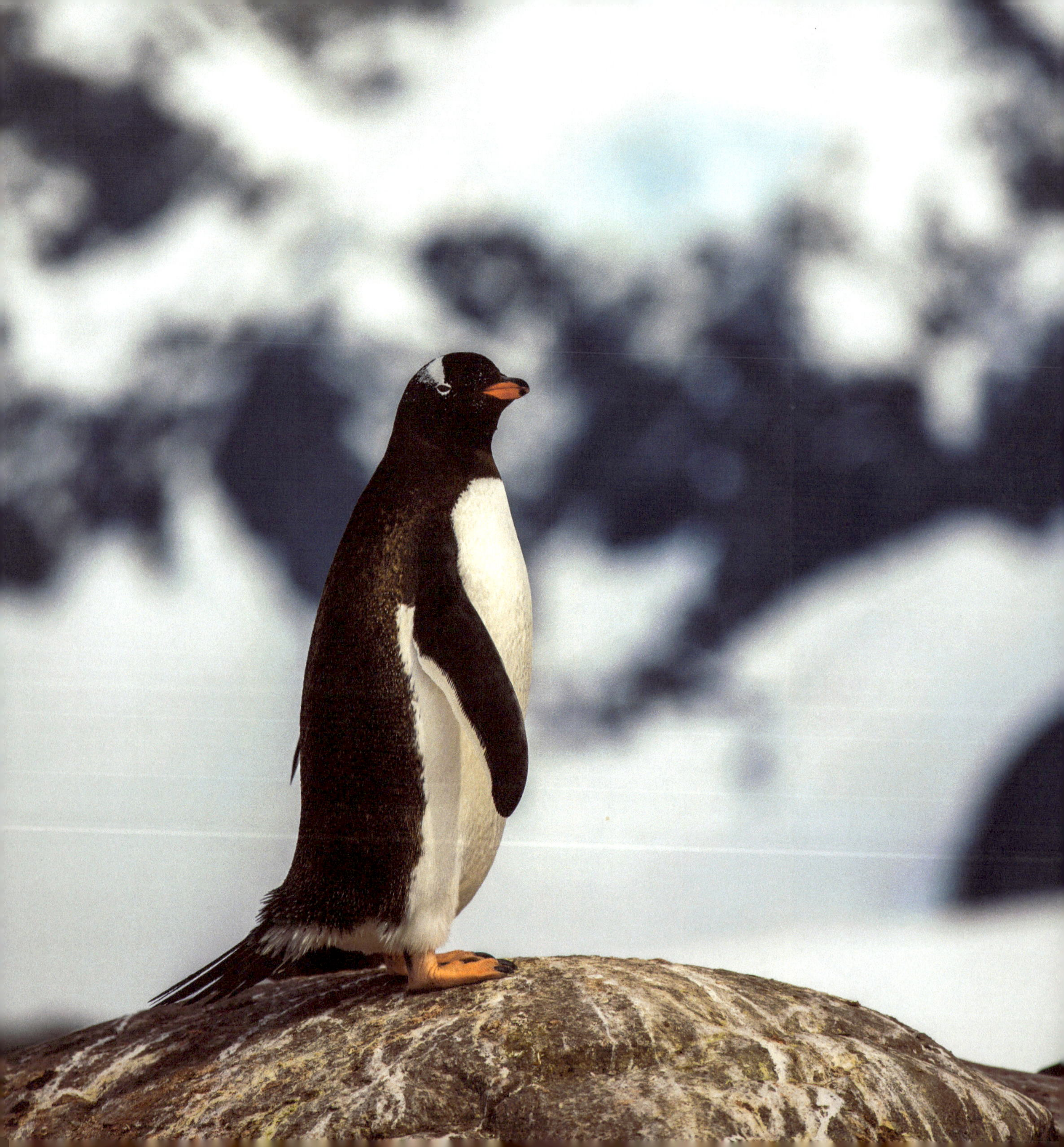

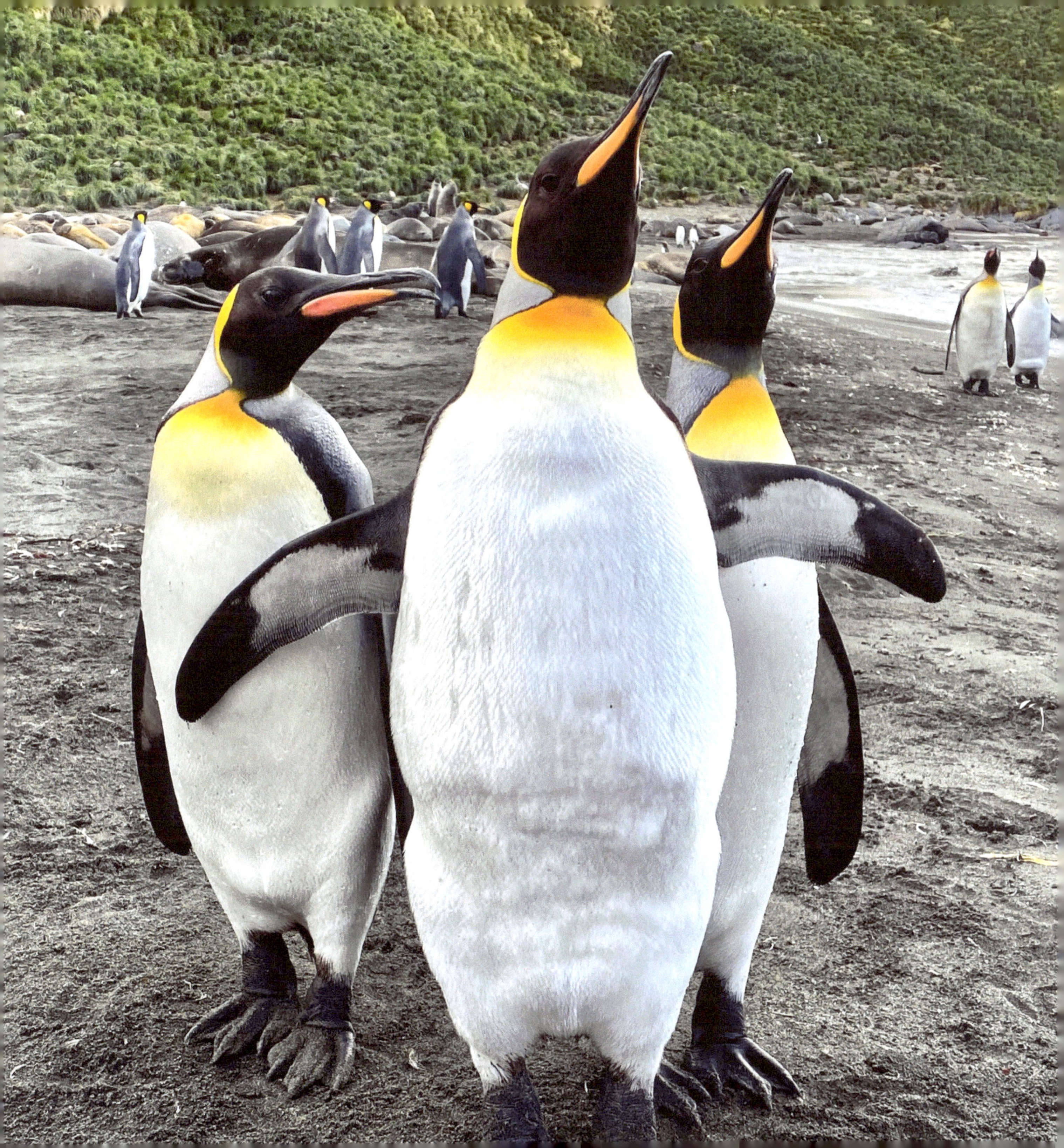

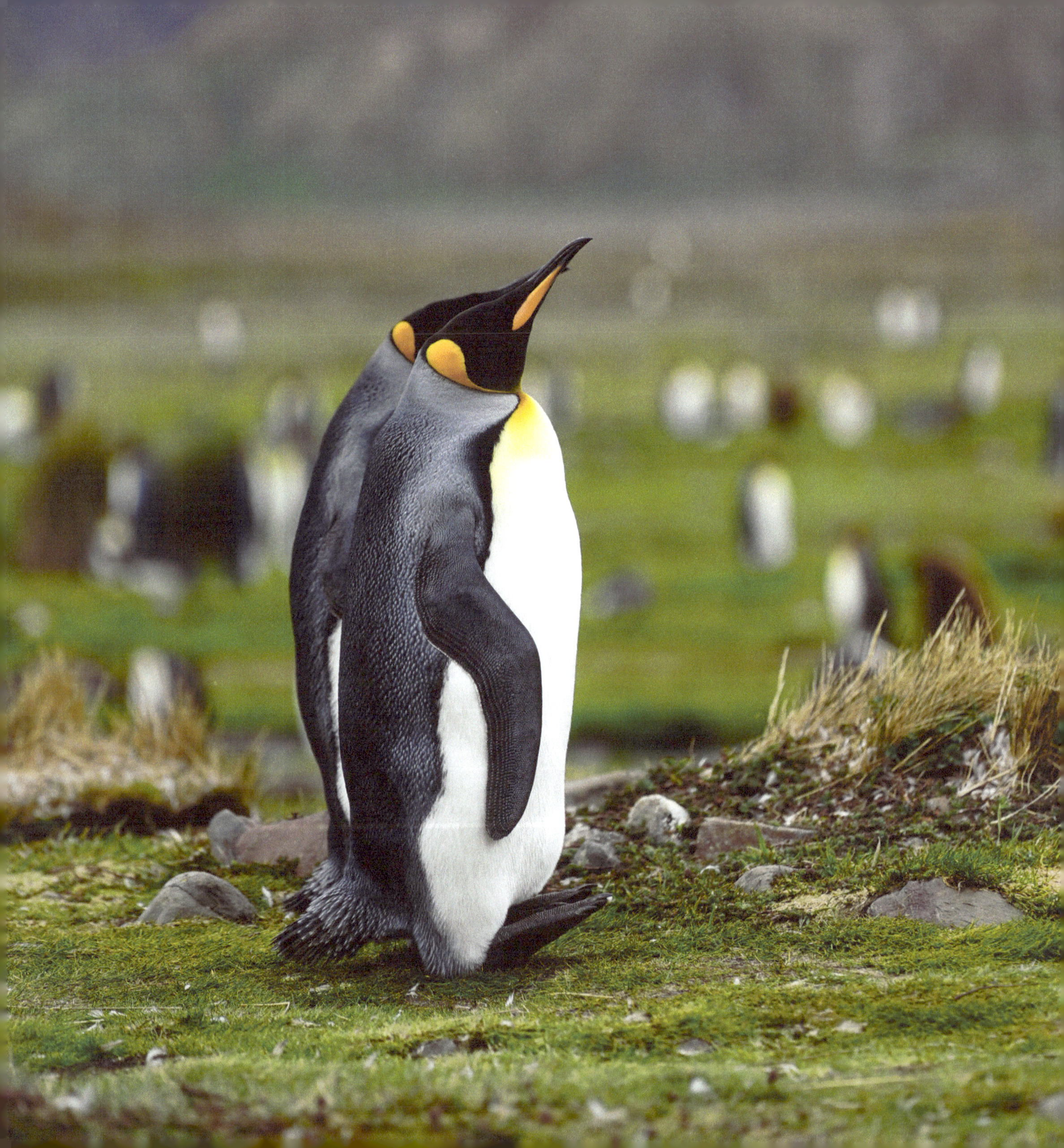

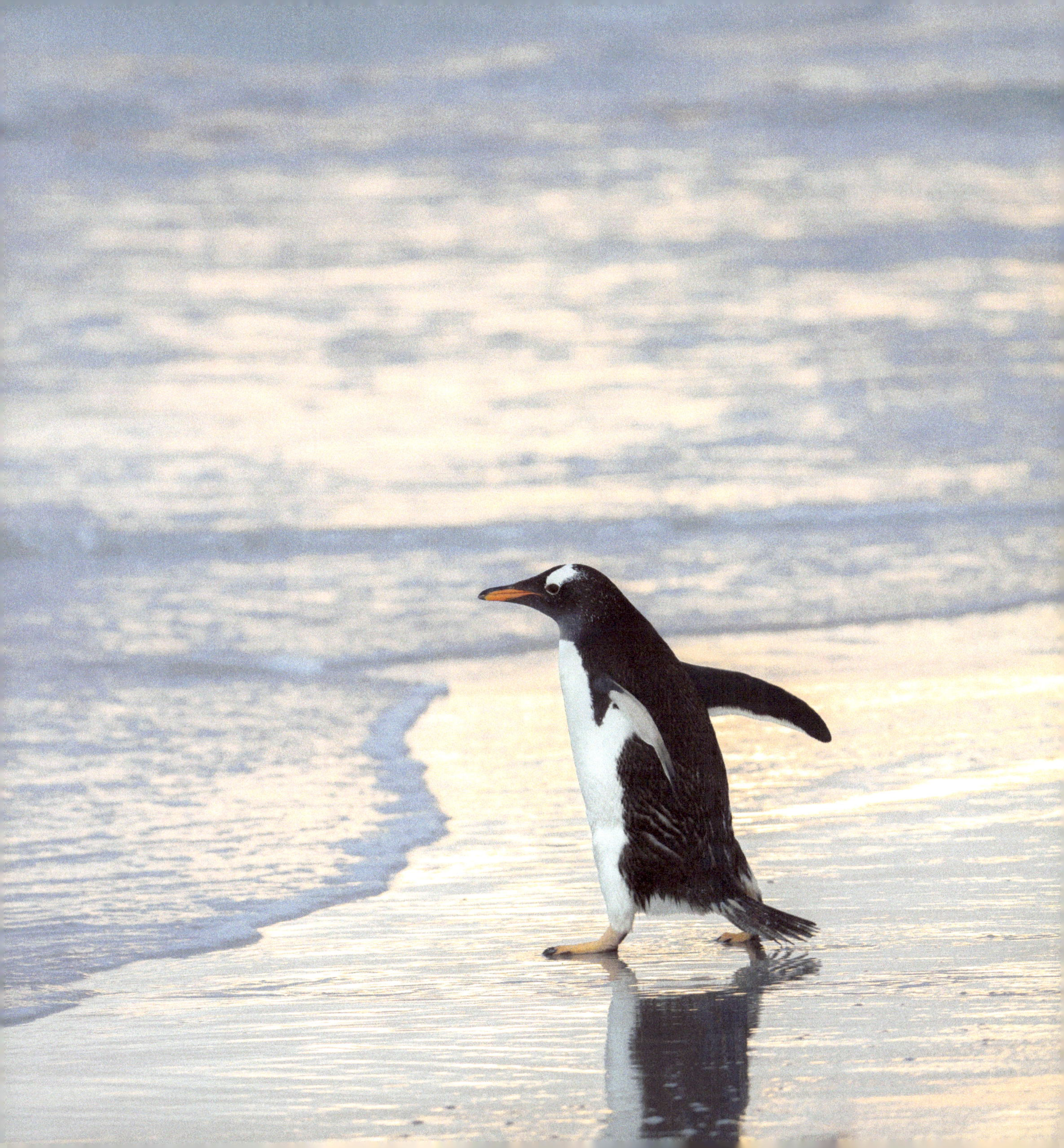

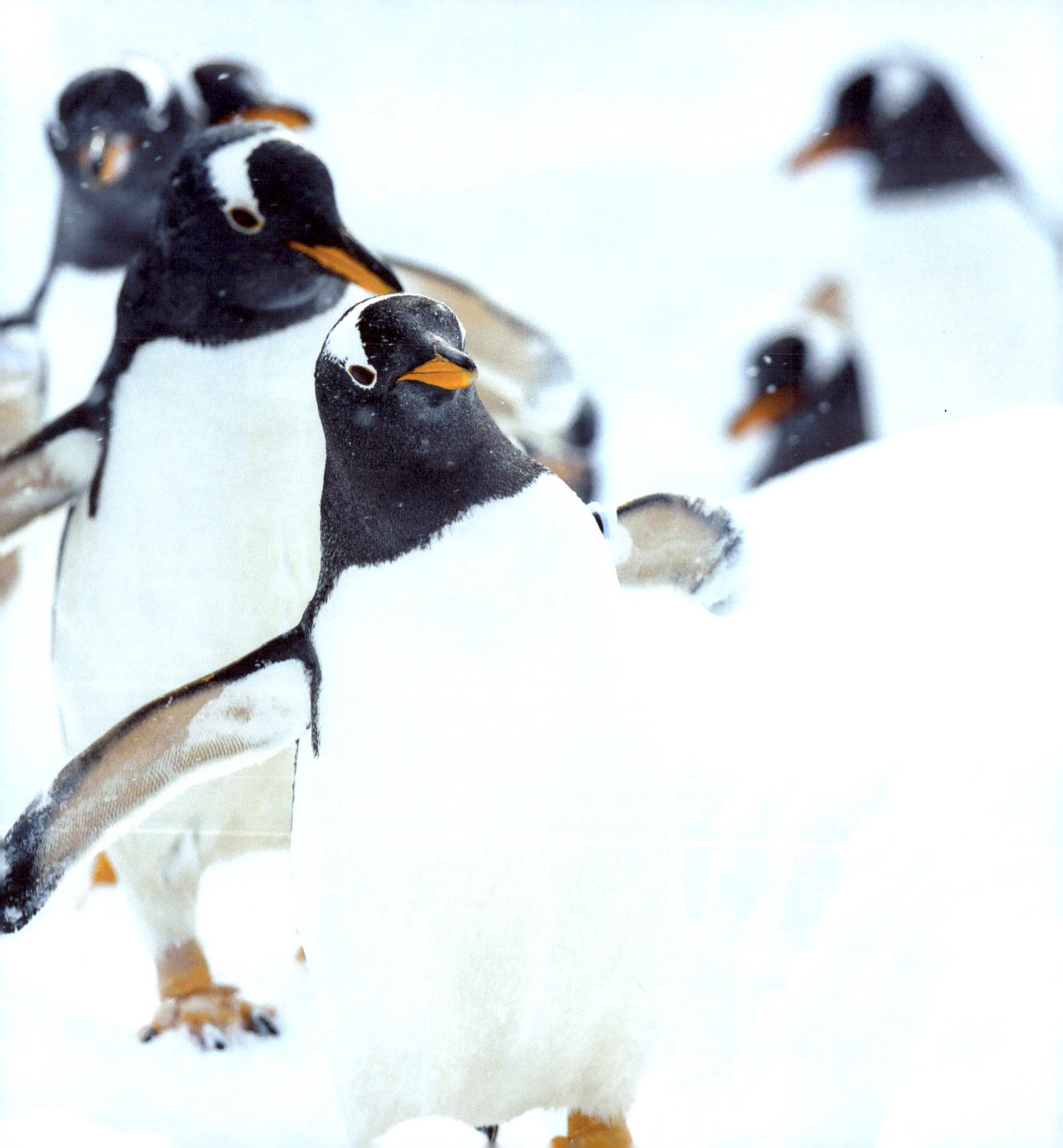

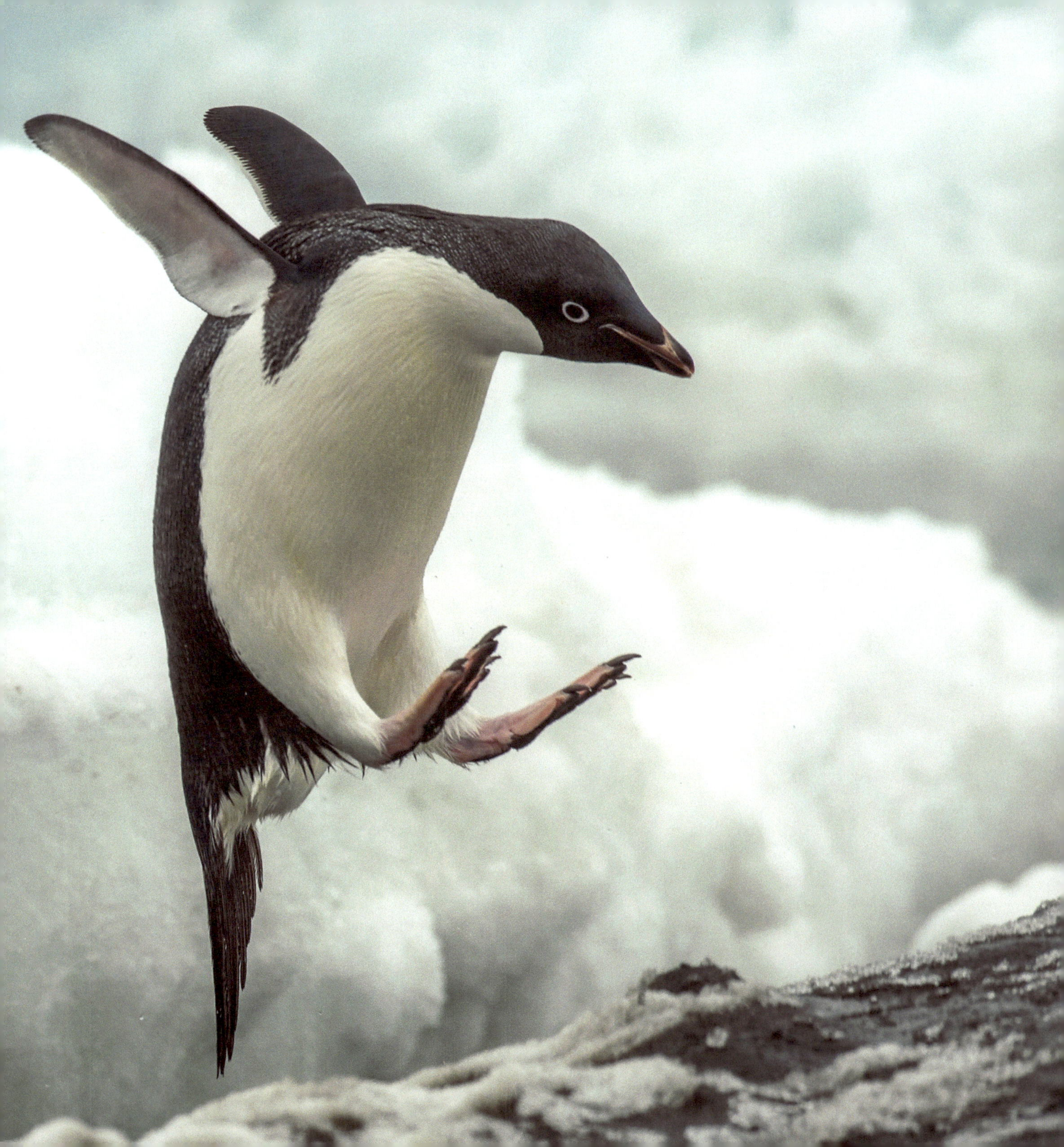

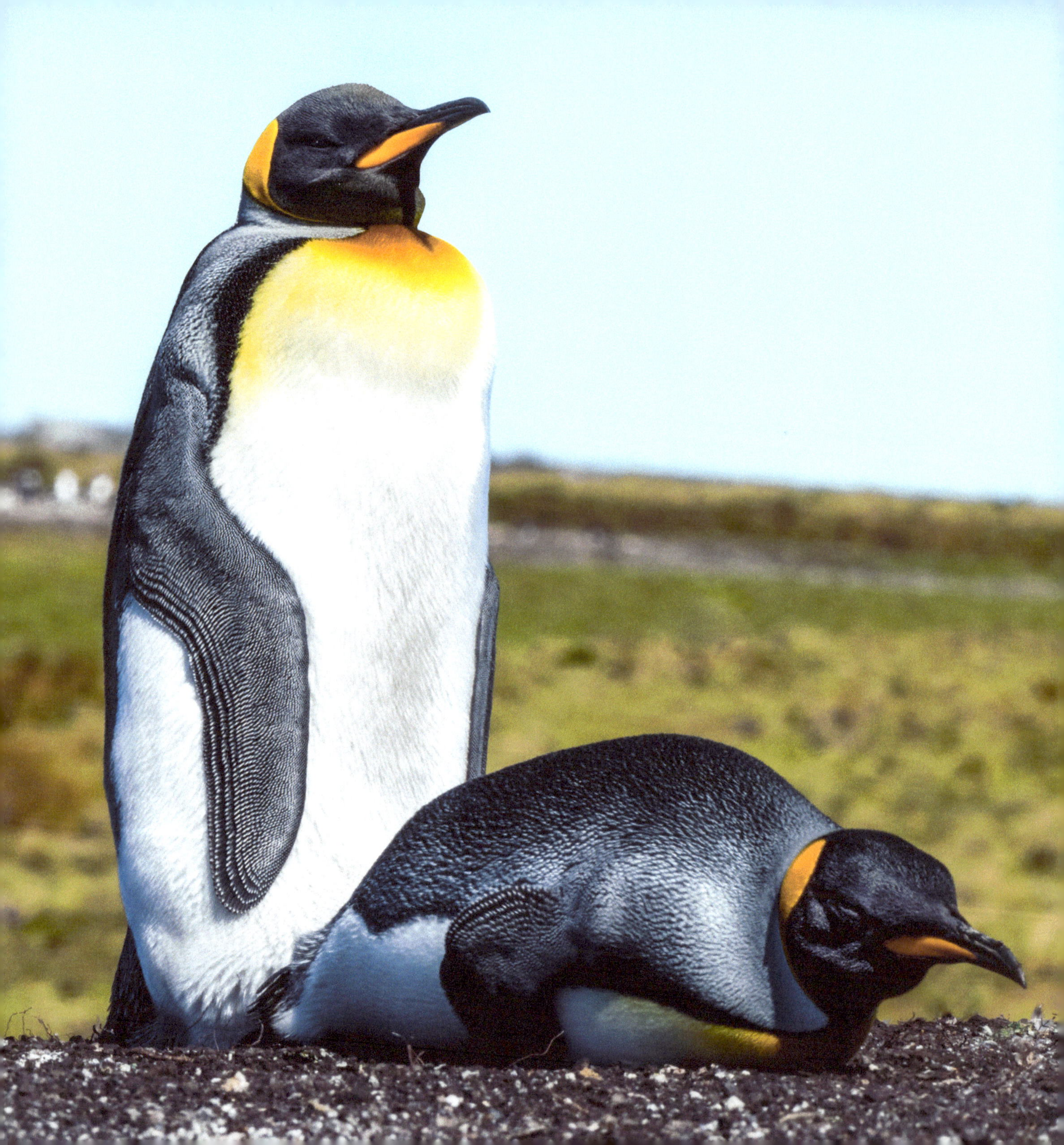

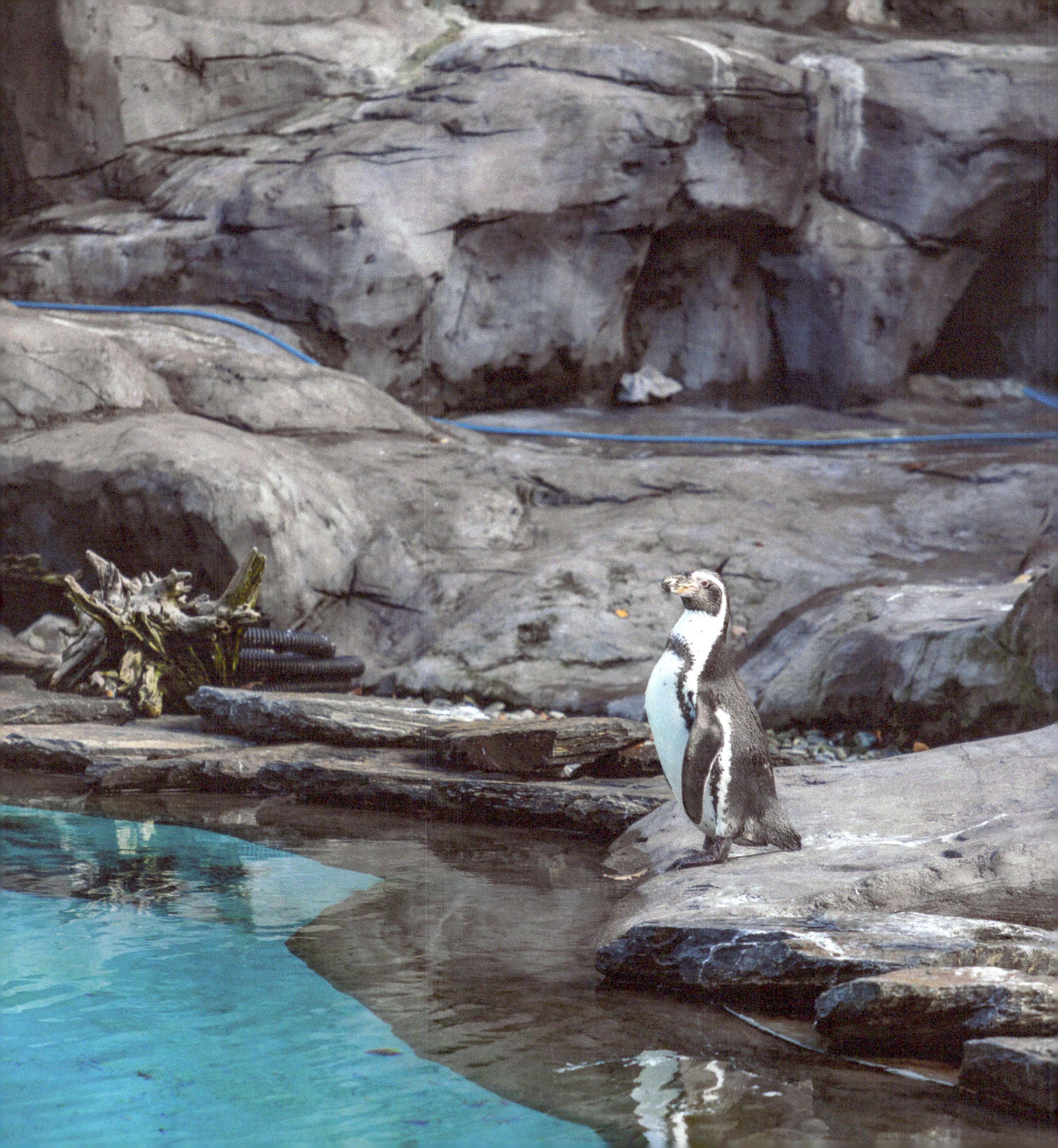

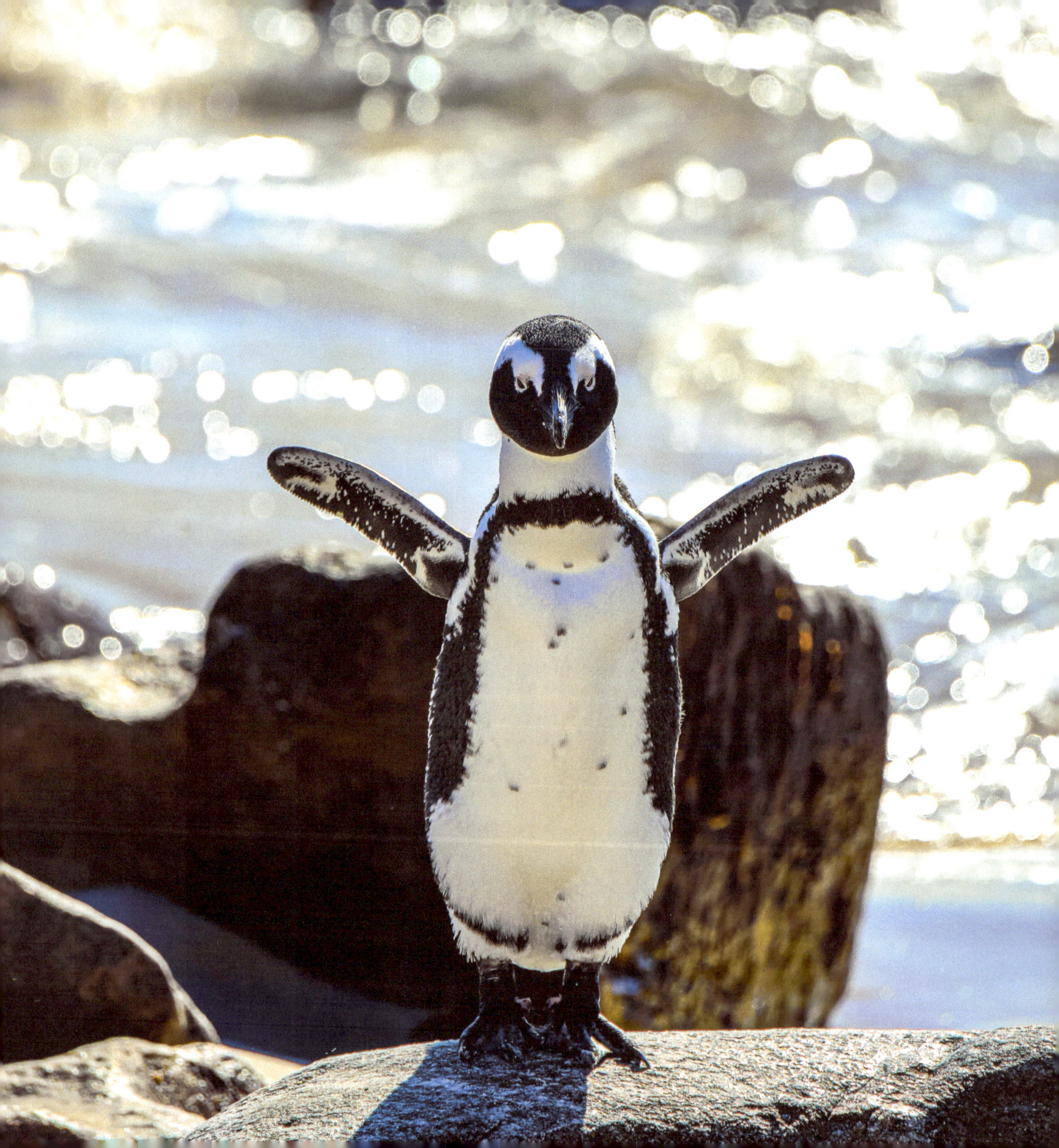

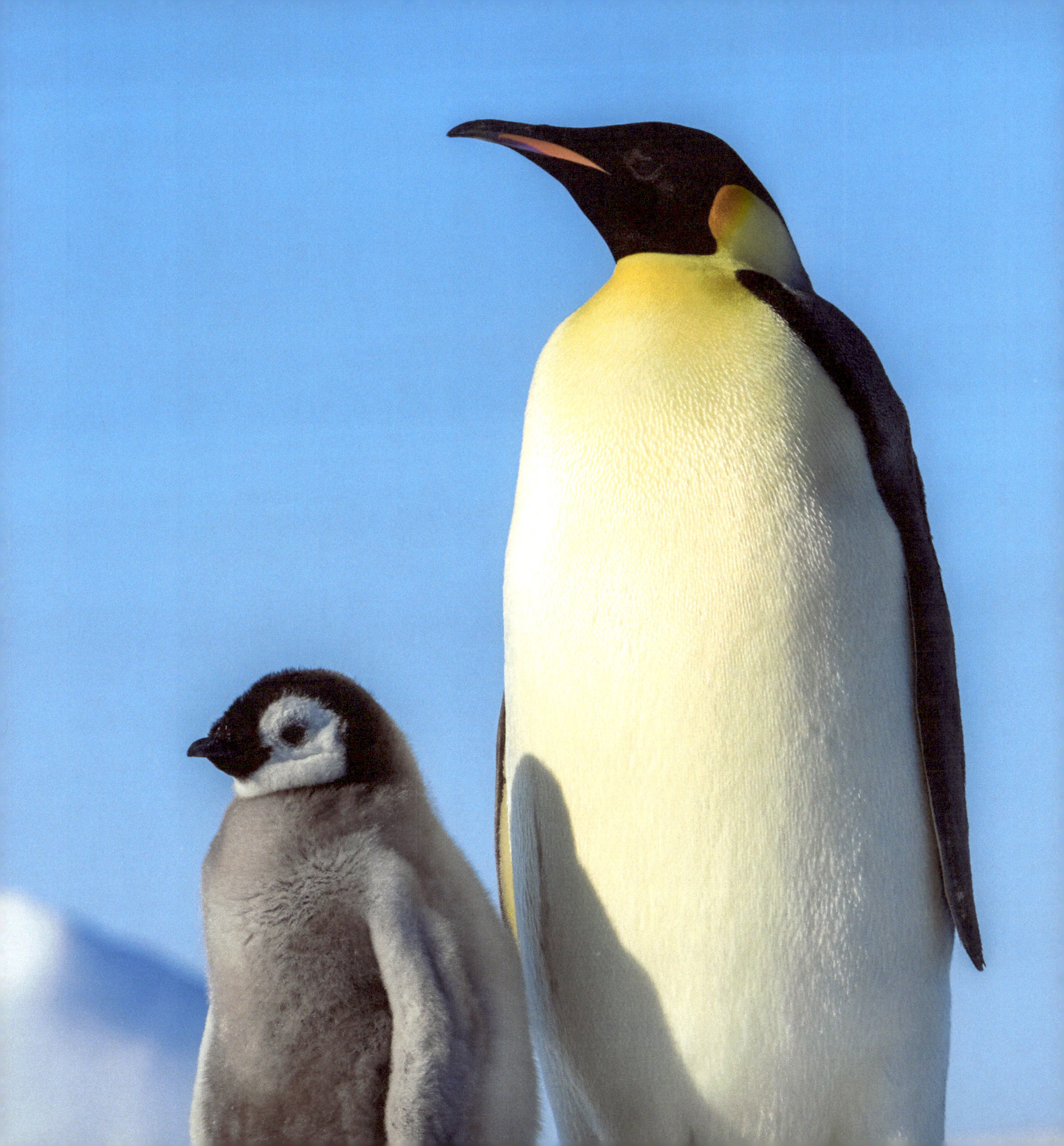

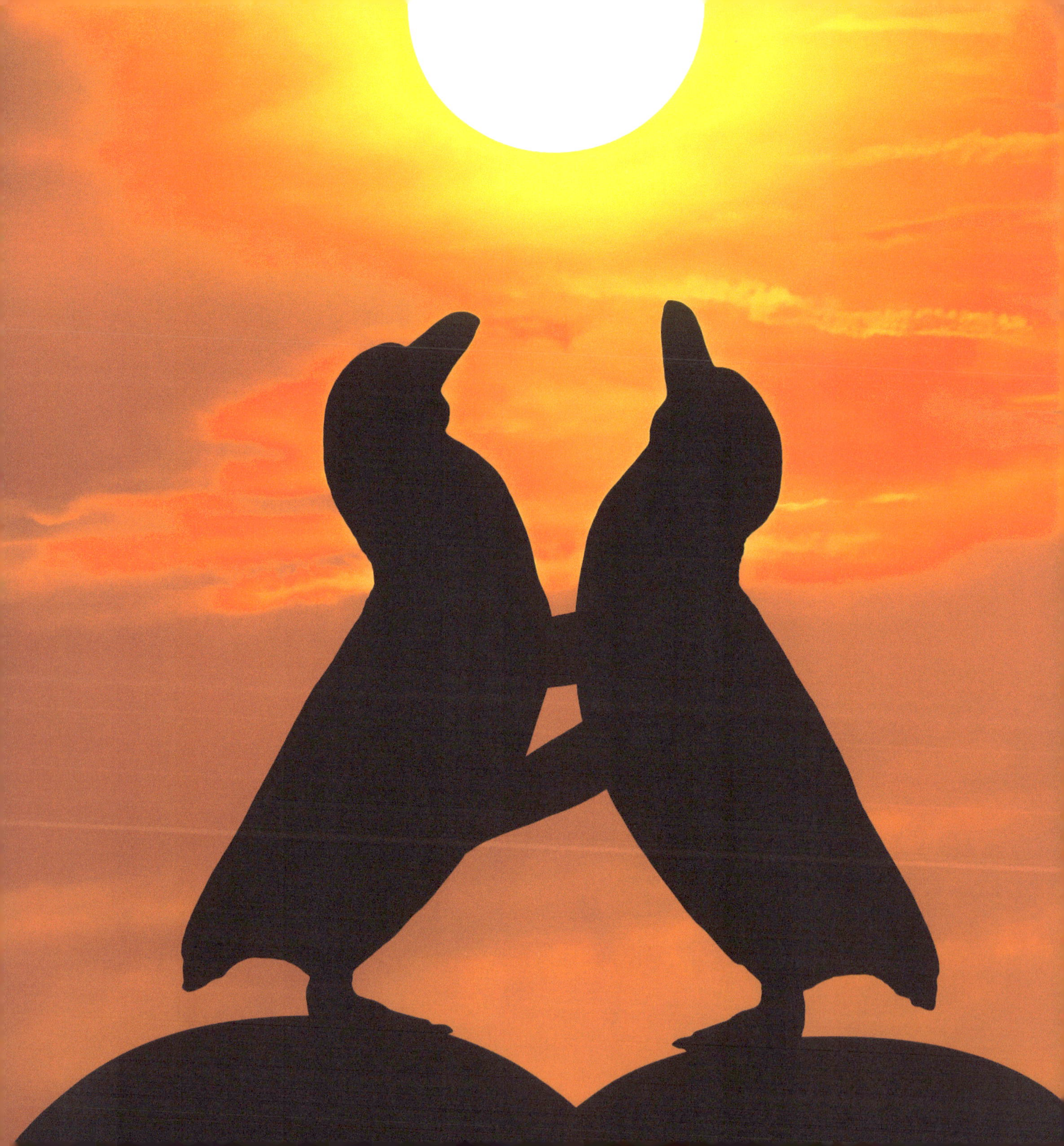

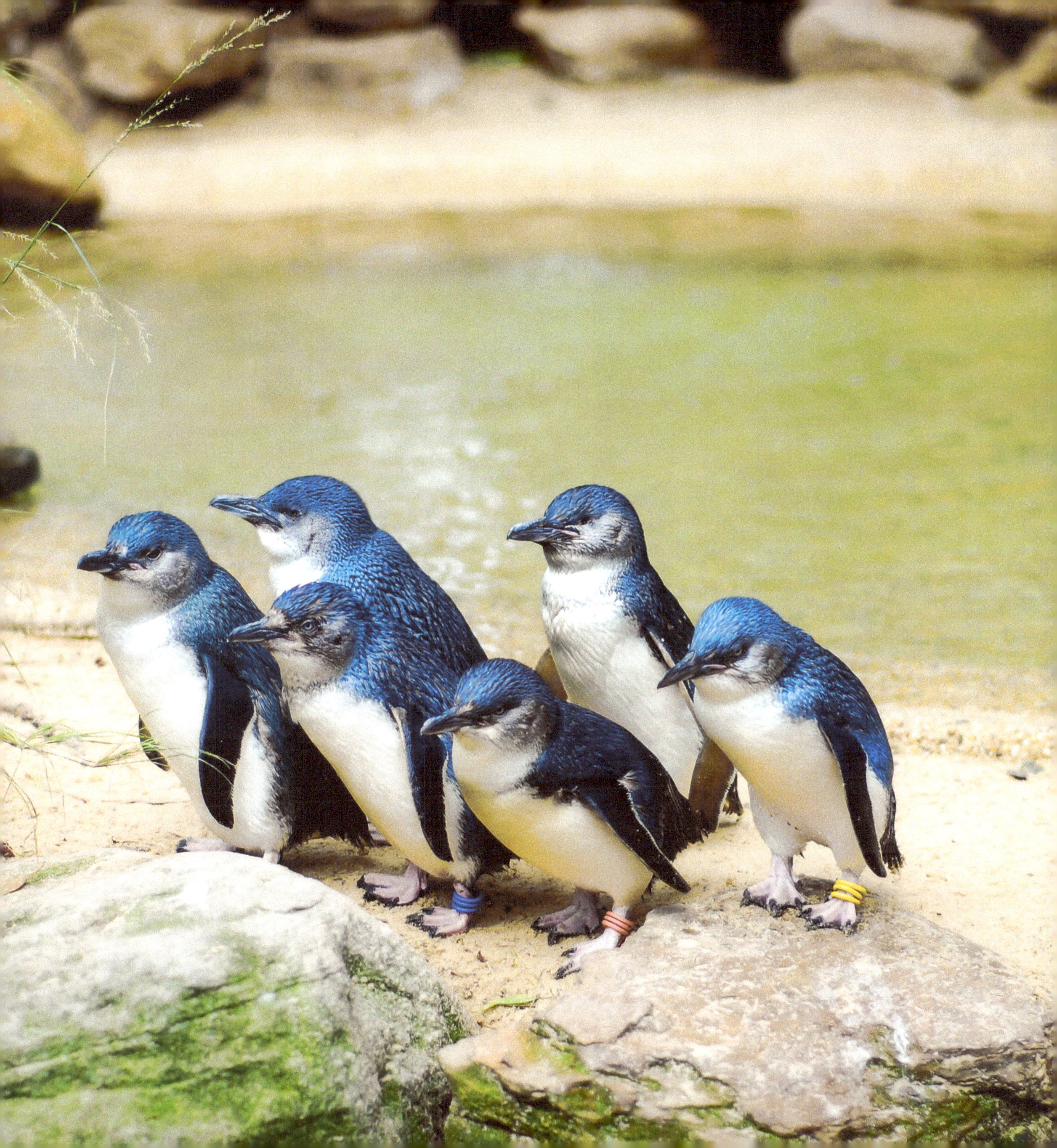

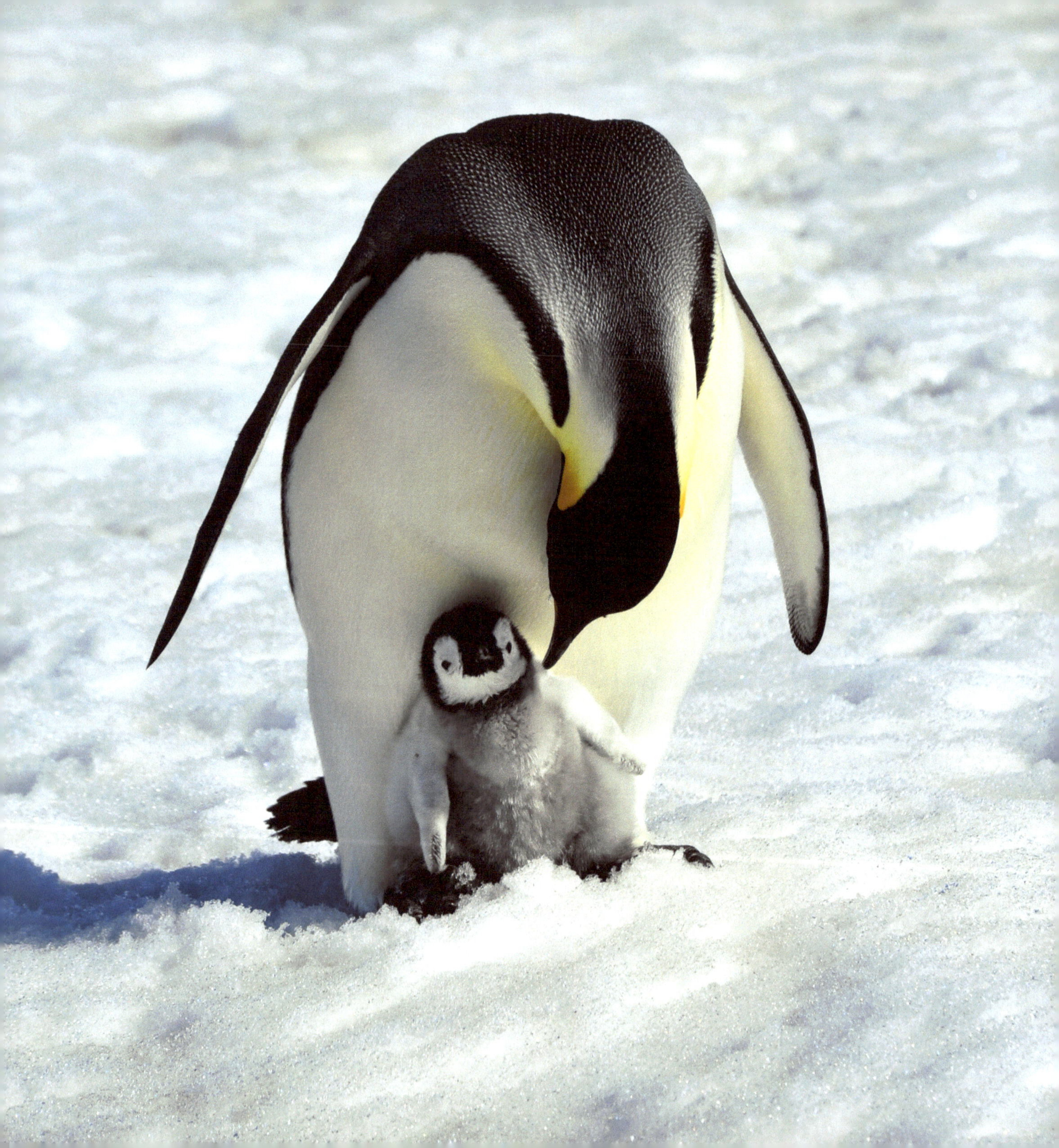

www.ingramcontent.com/pod-product-compliance
Lightning Source LLC
Chambersburg PA
CBHW040051240726
48664CB00004B/1143